Clergy
&
the
Sexual
Revolution

Ruth Tiffany Barnhouse

An Alban Institute Publication

The Rev. Ruth Tiffany Barnhouse, M.D., Fellow of the American Psychiatric Association and Episcopal priest, is Professor of Psychiatry and Pastoral Care at Perkins School of Theology, Southern Methodist University, Dallas, TX. She is author of many articles and books—among them *Identity* and *Male and Female* (with Urban T. Holmes).

TO THE MEMORY OF

James J. Young, C.S.P.
1940–1986

Jim was the Paulist priest who founded the National Conference of Separated and Divorced Catholics which has been so incalculably helpful. I worked with him in Boston in the early '70s, and we became good friends, maintaining contact over the years. It is fair to say that although I would certainly have been interested in sexuality anyway, it was working with Jim which really caused me to concentrate in this field as much and as soon as I did. He is a great loss to us all.

TABLE OF CONTENTS

The Publication Program of The Alban Institute is assisted by a grant from Trinity Church, New York City.

Library of Congress Catalog Card Number 86-73243

The Church and its leaders have had a long history of discomfort on the subject of sex. In the work of the Institute we continually run into situations in which there is either a conspiracy of silence, a set of rigid maxims, or on the other hand an empty-headed, value-less "anything goes" philosophy.

Such approaches give little help to young people and adults of both sexes who experience genuine confusion as they find themselves caught between powerful emotions and contradictory societal influences. In our work we find that confusion making life difficult in congregations and in religious organizations with which we are asked to consult. In the "old" days we often heard stereotypical and demeaning stories and jokes about "the pastor and the organist," "the priest and the boys in the choir." I remember a young clergyman who was known as "the petting parson." The jokes demeaned real people struggling in all kinds of situations, often with little help and they demeaned us as well. Today most of us have learned not to engage in the most blatant of these forms of gossip, but the anxiety remains. We often tend to hide the anxiety in speculation, rumor, and snide remarks.

That is not good enough—particularly today, when we have been experiencing a number of changes in our world that produce differences in how we relate to sex.

This book tries to give some help to those who are unwilling to settle for simplistic answers to a complex set of issues. Please do not expect to agree with everything in it, or even to *like* all of it. It is likely to touch you, as it does me, in areas in which I am not sure I really want to grow. Ruth Tiffany Barnhouse speaks directly, she minces no words. She believes, as I do, that sex is too important to be left in the hands of moral Ayatollahs or Hugh Heffners.

The readers of this book—clergy or lay—are people others come to for help and guidance. I believe this book can challenge you toward more clarity and, in the end, less anxiety. I hope it will lead you to be a better steward of your own sexuality, and that it will help you when people come to you for guidance.

Loren B. Mead

INTRODUCTION

How should clergy react to the sexual revolution? Should they simply exhort their flocks to hold fast to tradition? Should they coura-
geously lead their congregations to throw off the shackles of the
past and get "with it?" Would it be better to avoid public discussion
and just handle problems quietly case by case? Unfortunately, many
clergy have chosen one of these three options. None of them is sat-
isfactory. None really deals with the issues.

There is disagreement even in secular circles about the value of
the sexual revolution, and also about its implications for wider aspects of culture. Some well-known popularizers of nearly indiscrim-
inate sexual freedom have begun to backtrack. Erica Jong, for
instance, now says that traditional morality never died and that guilt
is common among those who adopted the new sexual freedom. In-
creasingly, people are having second thoughts about the once popular dictum "if it feels good, it must be right." As long ago as 1975 a
prominent sociologist and educator wrote that "people who make
their bodies the central focus of their existence will not be loving
to each other, but rather will be related in such a transient and
amoral manner as to cause each other much pain, if not outright
danger."[1] More recently a scholar asserts that ". . .a form of post-rev-
olutionary neo-puritanism has arisen as if many people, while not
denying the positive achievements of sexual liberation, were beginning to realize that in order to achieve anything important in life,
they needed to. . .channel the overflowing force of sexuality."[2] That
idea is in sharp contrast to the popular view of sexual activity as a
sort of psychological vitamin without regular doses of which one
risks the dangers of frustration and neurosis.

Clergy need to be aware of the rising tide of second thoughts in
the secular world. In the past they have vigorously resisted many
secular movements for a long time, finally capitulating only to discover that the secular winds are now blowing in a different quarter.
Needless to say, this does not enhance their credibility as serious

contributors to the formation of social policy. The tail does not wag the dog.

A crucial fact of great influence on secular second thoughts about the supposed advantages of unlimited sexual freedom is the rise in sexually transmitted disease. In the United States during 1985 there were over 5,000,000 new cases of such disease: 3,000,000 chlamydia, 1,000,000 papilloma, 900,000 gonorrhea, 350,000 herpes, 70,000 syphilis and 8,000 AIDS. According to the Public Health Service the next five years will see 270,000 Americans struck by AIDS, and there will be 54,000 deaths in 1991 alone, making AIDS the second leading cause of death.

In Africa, where the disease first appeared, AIDS is equally common in women and men. It is always fatal, and has now crossed the sex barrier in the United States, occurring for the first time in women who are not intravenous drug users nor recipients of transfusions. It is apparently accidental that its first appearance in this country was in homosexual men, and the rapid spread in that group depends on the high level of promiscuity which prevails there. But bisexual men have transmitted it to women, and it is also becoming frequent in prostitutes.

Each year 6,800 women in the United States die of cervical cancer. Such cancer has long been known to occur most often in promiscuous women or those who first had intercourse at an early age. But recent research now strongly implicates the papilloma virus as a cause of this disease. Herpes, though not fatal, is difficult if not impossible to cure. Researchers are working on vaccines and effective treatments for sexually transmitted diseases. So far nothing has succeeded.

Dr. George Kurman, an expert on papilloma virus, says "About the only advice we can give is to use condoms and get regular Pap smears."[3] He does not even consider the possibility of sexual continence. This is surprising, since many of those formerly very active sexually are now publicly discussing a change of life style. In the homosexual community this is particularly noticeable because casual encounters, formerly sought after, may now turn out to be fatal.

I am old enough to remember that before World War II the fear of venereal disease was a powerful tool in coercing young people to chastity. There were no sulfa drugs, no penicillin. Syphillis was progressive, eventually fatal. Children of syphilitic mothers were born with the essentially untreatable disease. Gonorrhea led to sterility, and complications of its infection were also often fatal. For forty years medical progress let us think that such dangers from sexual activity were a thing of the past. Now we are back where we started.

It would be a grave mistake for clergy to heave a sigh of relief, thinking that the resurgence of disease will effect a return to traditional sexual behavior. This overlooks the fact that vaccines against and treatments for the current scourges probably will be found. A new wave of sexual permissiveness could certainly follow such a development. If the issues are not examined now, clergy will once again find themselves fighting a losing rearguard action in the face of secular "progress."

What are the issues underlying the current sexual revolution? What are its advantages and disadvantages, real or apparent? What theoretical problems does it pose for clergy? What personal problems does it raise? What problems does it raise for clergy as leaders of their congregations? How can the church speak to these issues effectively? Are there any hard and fast rules governing Christian sexual conduct? If so, on what theological premises do these rules rest? If not, how are we to understand and come to terms with the Church's long tradition of having such rules?

These are not easy questions. Since anything to do with sex arouses powerful feelings, discussions of such topics often generate more heat than light. But the questions must be addressed, and this book will try to do so.

NOTES

1. Amitai Etzioni, "Is the Sexual Revolution Running Out of Steam?" *Medical Opinion, May, 1975, Vol. 4 #5.*

2. *Antonio Hortelano, "The Sexual Revolution and the Family" The Sexual Revolution*, eds.: Gregory Baum & John Coleman, Concilium 173 (3/1984).

3. Leslie Roberts, "Sex and Cancer" *Science '86*, July/August Vol. 7, No. 6, pp. 30-33, Published by American Association for the Advancement of Science).

CHAPTER I

What is the "Sexual Revolution"?

Background

What would you think of a society in which prostitution was public? In which the restrictions against it were harsh but generally ignored with the connivance of the authorities? In which young men congregated in bands, spending the evenings drinking, gambling, fighting with other gangs, terrifying ordinary people? In which rape was common and the victim often blamed? It sounds like the current scene in many large American cities but is actually a description of 15th century France. In the early 16th century there was a crackdown, and total moral freedom for men (it had been confined to men) was over. There was a call for renewed order in society, and the basis of such order was to be the family.[1]

When the monarchy was restored in England after the puritan excesses of Cromwell, the late 17th and early 18th century saw a period of extreme sexual permissiveness. The notorious Hellfire Club flourished, and the sexual practices of its aristocratic members included sado-masochism and everything else imaginable. Not only women, but children of both sexes were its frequent victims. Such excesses were of course not indulged in by everyone. Nevertheless, the sexual freedom available to the respectable general public was considerable. Not until the reign of Queen Victoria in the 19th century was there established firmly what we now think of as traditional sexual morality.

The sexual practices of our own ancestors, including many of the Founding Fathers, were considerably freer than we ever learned in history class. That is impossible to deny (though some have tried) since the results of at least some of their adventures were evident in the increasing numbers of black slave children who were clearly not 100% black.

We see, therefore, that ours is a revolution only in the mechanical sense—things which go round and round, frequently passing the same spot. But there is and always has been a considerable difference between publicly espoused standards of morality and what actually went on. Our libertarian age has taken great glee in publishing the secret diaries of eminent Victorians, showing that many were far from practicing what they preached. The foreword to a recent book on the history of Western sexuality says that what the reader "...will discover in that world hidden until very recently under the clinging, stifling folds of the mantle of respectability is a variety which can only fascinate. One of the most valuable lessons we are taught is that Christian doctrine, never uniform in any case, failed almost entirely to control western sexual expression."[2]

There is one important difference between our age and those of the past. Sexual rules, whether propounded by church or state (and until recently those two influences were seldom separated) were devised by men acting in a still intact patriarchal system. From the secular point of view, the rules were designed to ensure the orderly devolution of lineage and property. The religious point of view, while not denying the importance of such factors, had more abstract theological and ethical roots. From either point of view, women were always penalized more heavily than men for breaking the rules. Illegitimacy was undesirable from the secular side. From the religious side, it was obvious how difficult male sexuality is to control, and a common way of dealing with this was to put the blame for irregularities on women, the temptresses, without whose evil influence men would have been able to remain chaste. The new factor in our time is that the invention of effective birth control has made it possible for women at large (not just prostitutes) to be included in the current revolution.

This Round

The beginnings of the break with our immediate Victorian past occurred at the close of the first World War. That period was referred to as the "Roaring Twenties." In the 1928 edition of *Etiquette*, Emily Post included a chapter titled "The Vanishing Chaperone." Some of its contents, amusing to us, were radical innovations at the time. For instance, for the first time women could respectably travel alone. Nevertheless, if a gentleman accidentally met a lady he knew on a transcontinental pullman car, he was expected to get off at the next station and resume his trip on a later train in order not to compromise her reputation!

There had always been pornographic books, but traffic in them was underground. Serious authors often wrote such things, but published them either anonymously or under a pseudonym. In the '20s they began to write under their own name books which, while not pornographic by our standards, were far more daring both in content and vocabulary than our laws then allowed. These were published in foreign countries whose rules were less stringent. While not officially available at home, they were extensively discussed in literary journals, and the intelligentsia began to question their censorship.

The Great Depression and World War II then pre-empted everybody's attention. Following the war there was a strong resurgence of family life which had been so tragically interrupted. This characterized the 1950s in an exaggerated way since keeping women out of the workplace and training them to be avid consumers was deliberately engineered by Madison Avenue in order to prevent the country from slipping back into the Depression.[3]

But following the war, there also developed a revulsion against censorship since its abuses in Germany and Russia were so glaringly restrictive of personal freedom. Freedom is, after all, the cornerstone of the American value system, the foundation of our Constitution and Bill of Rights. Accordingly, citizens' groups such as the American Civil Liberties Union began a systematic attack through the courts on our censorship laws, and one by one these began to fall. This concern spread rapidly to the consideration of freedoms other than that of the press, and one liberation movement after another soon developed.

The publication of the Kinsey reports provoked a freer discussion of sex than ever before, and was accompanied by considerable surprise about what people actually do. The widespread assumption of many social scientists that what is normal may be deduced from what is frequent strongly influenced the discussion. Old standards were seriously questioned, particularly when they were promulgated on religious grounds. This was perceived as a violation of our cherished separation of church and state.

These factors together with the development of effective birth control methods culminated in the student uprisings of the 1960s. Here sexual freedom was seen as inseparable from other kinds of freedom, and the parietal rules in colleges and universities had to be abandoned. In most places this was followed by the establishment of co-ed dormitories. Couples then began to live together openly, with or without the intention of eventually marrying. These new customs rapidly spread to the general population. As women began to insist on their right to make all of their own decisions, especially about their bodies, the anti-abortion laws were challenged and eventually declared unconstitutional. The homosexual population understandably resented being the only group whose sexual freedom was still restricted and started their own liberation movement.

In the light of such developments, strict divorce laws seemed obsolete and unfair. The remaining stigma attached to divorce dissolved rapidly in most segments of society. Now that it was more easily available and no longer a disgrace, the divorce rate rose rapidly. The underlying misery in many marriages became evident, and this in turn increased the reluctance of children of such marriages to commit themselves to that institution, preferring instead some form of living together.

Apparent Advantages—Maybe Real

This section's heading is deliberately tentative. Since we are in the middle of social change, it is impossible to have either objectivity or the perspective of time. But there are some results of the sexual revolution which I find encouraging and which I hope will remain.

First, more realistic patterns of courtship are now possible. When I was a girl, the circumstances under which young men and women could meet were so artificial as to make it unlikely that they could get to know one another well enough to make an informed decision about marriage. One dressed up for dates and was on one's best behavior. Many topics were considered unsuitable for discussion, especially sex. This was true even if the couple engaged in what was then called "necking" or "petting." Young men and women both tended to see each other through the prevailing stereotypes rather than as distinct individuals.

Throughout society more casual dating patterns are now customary, patterns which encourage a more realistic approach to mate selection. Evidence comes from the college population. In 1975 a study was published of two groups of women students at Harvard, one group from a women's dormitory and the other from a dormitory integrated with men. The results showed that coresidency was a growth-producing experience for women by improving "the quality and appreciation of relationships with people of both sexes and the individual's confidence in herself as a person and as a woman." Coresidency was seen as offering "many more contacts with both men and women than does the one-sex dormitory and therefore far more opportunity to consider these issues in the context of real relationships. It offers greater opportunity for emotional growth."[4] In the years since that study was published, I have seen no evidence that it was in error, and much to confirm it. The one caveat is that not all young people, especially women, are ready for this experience. Single-sex dormitories should therefore continue to be provided for those who prefer them for whatever reason.

A second long overdue benefit of the sexual revolution is the erosion of the double standard. The ideal was always lifelong monogamy, but it was more or less tacitly accepted that men couldn't be expected to adhere strictly to that. Allowances were made for their weakness or virility, depending on how you chose to look at it. But this double standard entailed the existence of prostitutes, who were despised both by other women and by men. Such a division of women into good and bad while men were accepted no matter what, was obviously immoral, and one can only hope that it will never return. For reasons we shall consider later, however, prostitution is still with us, and weakening the double standard has brought new problems.

The removal of extreme social stigma from divorce and illegitimacy is also a welcome development. In the case of illegitimacy, lives could be ruined because of youthful error. The old shotgun wedding forced many doomed marriages. The alternatives were often worse. A child known to be illegitimate also suffered, and it is a real advance that it is no longer legal in most places to put that information on birth certificates.

Divorce often entailed social ostracism, people even being excluded from their churches. Great emphasis was laid on deciding who was the guilty party, and the "innocent" one was grudgingly readmitted to society. Ecclesiastical permission to remarry, if available at all, was restricted to those judged innocent. Change began in secular circles, reflected in such new legal concepts as "no-fault" divorce. But as anyone who has been through a divorce knows, that too is an error. No marriage irrevocably breaks down without some fault on both sides. "Shared-fault" would have been a more accurate designation.

As long ago as 1947 Dorothy L. Sayers wrote an essay in which she contrasted Christ's moral emphasis with ours. The secular concern with orderly devolution of private property was ecclesiastically supported by a narrow emphasis on sexual morality. Far too much weight was placed on "warm sins" while the church almost systematically ignored the "cold sins" of greed, exploitation and the like. That was because the continuation of those cold sins was essential to the economic and political systems. Sayers thought this alliance with Caesar was fatal to Christianity.[5] The sexual revolution along with other libertarian movements has forced the Church to rethink these issues. More cynically it can be noted that unless the policy of ostracism and condemnation had been abandoned, given the pres-

ent incidence of divorce and other sexual irregularities, church
membership would have declined even more disastrously than it
has. Regardless of how it came about, the more gracious attitude
must be welcomed.

Problems

Before the revolution the Church was perceived as judgmental and
guilt-producing in matters of sexual conduct. Unfortunately, this
perception was usually accurate. Therefore the Church did not take
the lead in any of the developments described above but reluctantly
took its cue from secular society when change was seen as inevitable. This sad fact importantly contributed to the severe problems
which the sexual revolution has brought with it. Most of these problems appear to be the result of the changes having emerged in the
context of a predominantly patriarchal, secular culture.

Elsewhere I have described the advantages to the human family
of the development, approximately 8000 years ago and all over the
world, of the patriarchal system. But we are now ready for something new, and the first stirrings of the movement to establish wom-
en's equality with men were felt about 200 years ago.[6] It seems to
be part of a general movement away from hierarchical and auto-
cratic forms of social organization toward something altogether
more egalitarian, the eventual form of which is still far from clear.
But it is well expressed in Galatians 3:28: "...there are no more dis-
tinctions between Jew and Greek, slave and free, male and female,
but all of you are one in Christ Jesus."

There are innumerable good and honorable men (and some
women too) who continue to believe that social stability depends
on retaining the old ways. In spite of that, there is no doubt that the
system is declining and has passed the point of no return. The remnants of the patriarchal system in an advanced state of decay are unfortunately among the strong influences affecting the shape of
sexual change, and some of the results are extremely ugly.

A grasp of the problems depends on understanding the difference between male and female sexuality. There is a strong tendency
for males to be primarily interested in the physical aspects of sex,
and this is especially pronounced in adolescence. One reason is
that for boys the changes of puberty begin at the physical level. The
spontaneous erection and the wet dream are universal male experi-
ences and usually occur entirely outside the context of any personal
relationship. A boy's sexual need is first experienced as purely physical, and it is only through the socialization process that he gradu-

ally learns to coordinate this need with the other values and
requirements of life.

In a traditional society, one where respectable girls would not
grant sexual favors before marriage, there were strong incentives
for the male to learn to control his sexual drive and to integrate it
with the rest of his personhood. For those occasions when his
drives overcame him, prostitutes were available. Sometimes the resort to prostitutes was altogether furtive, concealed from both parents and associated with shame. But often this outlet was accepted,
even sometimes actively encouraged, by the older generation of
men including the boy's father. Such lapses from ideal morality
were, however, entirely concealed from the women of the young
man's own family and class.

The custom of protecting respectable women from the knowl-
edge of how men really behaved was based on a variety of factors,
some of which (as much feminist literature has shown) served the
general patriarchal purpose of keeping women in second place. But
that custom also reflects an intuitive understanding of something
important about female sexuality.

For girls the physical changes of puberty (menstruation and
breast development) are not occasions of inescapable sexual arousal
but are seen as preparations for the possibility of motherhood.
What girls first experience in the sexual sphere is the wish for emotional connection with boys. If they are raised to believe that the
best way to relate to boys is to be sexually unavailable, then that is
what they do. If they are socialized in a milieu which is sexually
permissive, they will conclude that the best way to form the desired
relationships is to be sexually available. In either case the recognition of their own specifically sexual needs and responses usually
has to be learned. Nature does not force these lessons on them in
any obvious way as it does for their brothers. Thus in adolescence
sexuality is not integrated but is dissociated in both girls and boys,
boys tending to over-physicalize it and girls tending to over-emo-
tionalize it.

Victorian customs prevented respectable women from maturing
past this point, encouraging them to think of sex as a deplorable
necessity for men. In order to be perceived as desirable husbands,
men had to downplay their own sexuality in front of women. They
were granted some leeway during youth, but this was thought of as
"sowing wild oats" and they were expected to grow out of it. Such
customs had the virtue of forcing men to integrate their sexuality to
some extent. Manhood, under those conditions, was not defined
primarily in terms of sexual prowess.

Things have changed. Instead of being (at least publicly) a transient period of "sowing wild oats," the immature, dissociated sexuality of adolescent males is now presented as a desirable standard for adult men. Hugh Hefner's "Playboy Philosophy" brought this kind of sexuality out of the closet and now, only a quarter of a century later, his initial efforts seem tame almost to the point of innocence by comparison with what has since developed. The depersonalization of sex has become extreme. William Thompson, formerly a professor of history at MIT, convincingly argues that this is related to our technological society. His description is worth quoting at length:

"Since few men willingly suffer their own dehumanization, industry and technology have found that an appeal to sexuality is one very efficient way of camouflaging the internal and external dehumanization. The industrial quality of sexuality is...clearly in evidence in the ads in *Playboy*...In a penthouse apartment that is a technological paradise of stereos, tape recorders, cameras, blenders, automatic bars and electric beds, the sleek air-brushed nude that offers enjoyment without involvement is the ideal appliance of any young engineer's dream. Producing sensations without sentience, the female represents what every trained technologist desires. He is free to dismiss everything that his culture tells him to, and still be safe from the exposure that personal involvement with a real woman might contain."[7]

Sex without involvement is still the ideal in too many quarters. A strong feature of the sexual revolution was the liberation of women. They were to claim their sexual rights along with men. But too many women fell for this line, not recognizing that they were only being given permission to act like immature men had under the old double standard. Libertine behavior was no longer confined to men and prostitutes. What this accomplished was to give men for free what they formerly had to pay for, and to make it much more accessible. Without efficient, cheap birth control this development would not have been possible.

Nobody thought about whether these developments met the real needs of women. But twenty years ago, when these changes began, feminists did not want to admit that there were any differences between men and women, fearing that any such admission would be interpreted as female inferiority. They were still accepting men as the standard for all human beings, and were pathetically determined to match that standard. In the last few years, however, the tide has turned and there is now general recognition that men and women do differ in important respects.[8] It can now be seen that the supposed sexual freedom did offer some benefits. But women were again being taken advantage of, although in a new way. Their right to say "no" to a sexual advance was severely inhibited by the probable consequences: no more dates. And, as we saw, women do want emotionally satisfying relations with men. Many have been willing to be sexually compliant in order to achieve that goal.

Unfortunately, the excessive focus on the physical aspects of sex at the expense of the relational ones was given further impetus by the new discipline of sexology. One of the original Kinsey team wrote about adultery as follows: "The greatest danger of the affair that is undertaken solely for variety's sake is the possibility of becoming emotionally involved. The purely physical aspect of an affair does not represent a threat to marriage, but the emotional aspect does."[9] He is unaware that in truly mature people—even men!—the physical and emotional are not really separable. A recent thoughtful critique of sexology by Andre Béjin points out that the scientific authority of its experts comes from definitions of sexual well-being which arise out of laboratory research. All persons capable of achieving orgasm at will are considered to be in good health. This simplistic view of sexual satisfaction he calls "orgasmological behaviorism" and notes that it favors hedonism. Commenting on Masters' statement that "orgasm is an entirely egocentric affair," he says that if that were true, the partner is merely "the helpful parasite in a fundamentally autoerotic act."[10]

As long ago as 1968 the psychoanalyst Dr. Natalie Shainess saw clearly the reductionistic fallacy inherent in the methods of sex research. Her views made her very unpopular with many of her distinguished male colleagues, but time has shown that she was right. She noted that sexual problems persisted in spite of sexual freedom. She related this to the increased alienation and mechanization of our culture and said that Masters and Johnson were part of this by overextending the physiological aspects of sexual response to cover the entire realm of sexuality. Their major false premise was the assumption that studying sexual responses only biologically could offer meaningful information. "What Masters' research studies is 'output,' the final pathway, and from this about all one can learn is that something is wrong. To find out what is wrong, it is necessary to study 'input.'. . .Treatment relates to what lies between the two—the processing. And humans can be sexually adequate in one situation and not in another." She also questioned the normality of the responses obtained under laboratory conditions of prolonged overstimulation and suggested that we should ". . .avoid the dehumanizing rape of sex and strive to understand the failure in ability to love freely." Noting the new sexual egalitarianism between men and women, she saw that too often "sexual activity is seen or experienced as competitive action rather than a potentially powerful bond of reciprocal giving."[11]

A colleague of mine reported the case of a woman who had been carefully screened psychiatrically before going through Masters and Johnson's sex therapy. But after this was "successfully" concluded, she developed a full-blown case of paranoia. For women especially, sexual response is an indicator of the state of the relationship, and this function needs to be maintained. Thus treating the sexual dysfunction alone is like treating a fever by redesigning the thermometer. If Carl Jung is right, and sex itself is a symbol of wholeness, then to teach people to manipulate that symbol to an extent which confuses their perception of the state of the underlying wholeness is indeed to invite psychological disaster. Of course both men and women might have this reaction, but women would probably have it more often since for them sex is less likely to be an end in itself.

I have emphasized the errors in sex research because in my experience clergy are frequently intimidated by scientific experts and often accept their statements without critical examination. It is important to check their underlying assumptions which are not intrinsically scientific, but which may skew not only their research design but the conclusions which they draw from the facts they uncover. Nevertheless, I do not want to obscure the real advantages to everyone in making sex a discussable topic. Some readers may be old enough to remember the tragedies associated with its shameful hiddenness in the past, especially problematic for women who often knew almost nothing about their own bodies and had been taught to think that sexual pleasure was not quite nice. There is a place for sex research, and this is well described by the philosopher Irving Singer: "The new sexology. . .may eventually succeed in combining the precision of science with the greater sensitivity to human differences which often appears in the humanistic tradition. . .Without the methods of scientific investigation, the humanities founder in loose generalizations, which may easily turn into dogmatic beliefs showing none of that sensitivity to which I referred. Without the immersion in everyday reality which the humanities take as their province, the life sciences lose their relevance to life itself and often blur the differences between individual responses."[12]

The whole culture has been pathologically hypersexualized, and the concept of friendship has been seriously eroded. Any intimacy is assumed, at least feared, to be sexual no matter what the sex of the participants. But friendship is a relationship of equality. The sexual attitudes of today do not favor equality since they assume that the goal of the encounter is personal satisfaction in which the partner is to be used rather than truly met. This attitude results from the problems of the sexual revolution which, as we have seen, stem from the glorification of a pattern of male sexuality which is fundamentally immature, from the harm done by encouraging women—against their natural inclination—to imitate this pattern, and from the excessive focus on the physical aspects of sex at the expense of the relational aspects.

Thus the decadent remains of patriarchy socialize men to experience their manhood in terms of two questionable premises. The first is their need and their right to free sexual expression essentially dissociated from relationship let alone commitment. The second, a holdover from former times, is that they are superior to women and should aim as far as possible to be in control of any situation in which they find themselves. Dominance and real relationship are fundamentally incompatible in contemporary society, which is inexorably (if with difficulty) moving toward egalitarian systems of social organization.

All men in this culture have been socialized this way. There are, of course, many maturing and civilizing influences as well. These protect many—one hopes, most—men from being exclusively formed so dangerously. But there are frightening indicators to the contrary. There is a serious rise in violence against women and children. The boundary between liberation and exploitation has been crossed. There is an alarming rise of both rape and incest. It is estimated that in this country there are at least one million women survivors of incest with their fathers, and more have suffered at the hands of other male relatives. The connection between sex and violence is clear in the case of a woman whose father used to rape her as a form of punishment for disobedience. That father was a pillar of his church.

In an article well worth reading in its entirety, Susan Hanks explores the problem. "Under the rhetoric of sexual liberation and freedom of the press, pornography explicitly links sex and violence. Women are raped, tortured, mutilated, bound, etc., as a way of sexually stimulating male characters. The violence of these acts is trivialised by presenting women as enjoying being abused. This has escalated in recent years to the production of 'snuff' films—so called because the actresses are actually murdered in front of the camera to. . .provide sexual stimulation for the viewers."[13] Not only women but children also receive this kind of treatment, including murder. Pornography is now a multi-billion dollar business—and still growing. In spite of sexual freedom for all, prostitutes stay in business partly because they will permit acts of violence and degradation which men's social acquaintances will not.

In ordinary society the overtones of this violence are reflected in common language. In the old days, to "make a pass at" a woman was the phrase used for a sexual overture. Now the expression is to "hit on" her. And in one college survey nearly 70% of the men said that they would like to commit rape if they thought they could avoid being caught.

Many have wondered why such violence against women, child prostitution, and "kiddie porn" are now so prevalent. But if men are fixated at an adolescent level of sexuality and also imbued with the need to dominate, it is not surprising that they express this through violence toward their sex partners. And some still adolescent men will feel that they cannot be sexually superior to anyone but children.

Clergy should not be quick to assume that members of their flock are surely not involved in anything so dreadful. They would be surprised if they knew how many men in their congregations sneak into "adult" bookstores or "adult" movies, at least when away from home. And many a household contains copies of *Hustler* or *Penthouse* if only in the bathroom. This is the kind of thing the pastor, along with wives and children, will be the last to hear of.

In this chapter we have briefly considered the history of the sexual revolution. We have seen that it does bring some gains, especially in our ability to be straightforward and realistic about sex, and to be charitable to those caught in various sexual irregularities. There is in many quarters real promise that men and women are more easily able to relate to one another as responsible equals. But the secular base of much of the change has promoted an immature concept of sexuality based on adolescent masculinity. The harm to women is obvious. The harm to men is just as great even though society tends to gloss it over. There is a real task before clergy as they attempt to deal with these issues both personally and professionally.

NOTES—CHAPTER I

1. Jacques Rossiaud, "Prostitution, Sex and Society in French Towns in the Fifteenth Century" In *Western Sexuality: Practice and Precept in Past and Present Times*, eds., Philippe Aries & Andre Bejin, trans. Anthony Forster. (Oxford: Basil Blackwell, 1985).

2. Peter Laslett, Foreword to *Western Sexuality: Practice*....

3. Betty Friedan, *The Feminine Mystique*, (Englewood Cliffs, N.J.: Prentice-Hall, 1963). See especially Chapter 9, "The Sexual Sell."

4. Elizabeth Aub Reid, M.D., "Effects of Coresidential Living on the Attitudes, Self-Image and Role Expectations of College Women" (*American Journal of Psychiatry*, May 1974).

5. Dorothy L. Sayers, "Christian Morality" *Unpopular Opinions*, (New York: Harcourt Brace and Co., 1947).

6. Ruth Tiffany Barnhouse, "Patriarchy and the Ordination of Women" *The Saint Luke's Journal of Theology/cf1, (September 1975), Vol. XVIII, No. 4*

7. *William Irwin Thompson, At the Edge of History*, (New York: Harper Colophon, 1972).

8. Carol Gilligan, *In A Different Voice*, (Cambridge: Harvard University Press, 1985). This was chosen as an example precisely because it is not written from the Jungian point of view. It comes from the mainstream of psychology today. Jungians have always insisted on a distinction between masculine and feminine. Readers wishing to examine the question from the Jungian point of view are referred to the work of Ann Ulanov and John Sanford.

9. Wardell Pomeroy, "Sex Boredom in Marriage Can Be Helped by Counseling" *Clinical Psychiatry News*, (December 1975), Vol. 3, No. 12.

10. Andre Béjin, "The Influence of the Sexologists and Sexual Democracy" *Western Sexuality* (see note 1 above).

11. Natalie Shainess, M.D., "The Problem of Sex Today" *American Journal of Psychiatry*, (February 1968, Vol.124:8).

12. Irving Singer, *The Goals of Human Sexuality* (New York: W.W.Norton & Co., 1973).

13. Susan Hanks, "The Sexual Revolution and Violence Against Women: The Boundary Between Liberation and Exploitation" *The Sexual Revolution*, eds.: Gregory Baum & John Coleman, *Concilium* 173 (3/1984).

Though not specifically cited in this chapter, the following two books can shed considerable light on the issues:

Ruth Tiffany Barnhouse, *Identity*, (Philadelphia: Westminster Press, 1984).

Mark Gerzon, *A Choice of Heroes: The Changing Face of American Masculinity* (New York: Houghton Mifflin, 1982). This book is particularly valuable since it discusses contemporary issues about masculinity from a male point of view on the basis not only of the author's experience, but a number of interviews with men conducted over 10 years' time.

CHAPTER II

Problems in Thinking About the Sexual Revolution

Starting Point

Too many clergy are behind the starting line for clear thinking about the sexual revolution. There are several reasons for this, not all of which apply to all clergy. And there are a growing number who have for the most part managed to stay out of these traps. In some cases the difficulties lie not so much in actual clerical beliefs and attitudes as in the ways society tends to stereotype clergy. If these are kept in mind, misunderstandings can often be prevented.

Few branches of the church have admitted women to ministry until recently, and all are still heavily patriarchal in the upper echelons of the hierarchy. To the extent that they believe in the intrinsic value of the patriarchal system, ministers will have trouble understanding many of the phenomena of the sexual revolution, especially those features which are conditioned by the women's liberation movement. Those who are benevolent patriarchs of the old school may have trouble recognizing the fact that most manifestations of patriarchy remaining in this country are decadent, and are directly responsible for the ugliest aspects of the revolution. It will be hard for them to understand what Hanks means when she writes about her hopes for the future: "Hopefully, this process will minimize the culturally acquired projections, assumptions and distortions many men and women have of each other. Dispelling these myths will minimize the polarization of men and women in the patriarchal culture which lays the foundation for the violence against women."[1]

Clergy often have little credibility with secular policy makers in a world which views idealism as soft, not really practical, especially not in a political or economic crisis. In some quarters even male clergy are stereotyped as prudes, possibly not even real "he-men" even though their profession is heavily—in some denominations exclusively—male. This should convince them that they really have a job to do in a culture where too many people think that when "real" men get by themselves, they use bad language, show contempt for women, boast of having got the better of opponents by fair means or foul, and of having exploited their inferiors. The respectful silence with which a minister's remarks are frequently met should be viewed with suspicion. It may not even reflect understanding, much less agreement.

The Church's history of unrealistic overemphasis on sexual sins as the worst of all is no help. Even if a particular pastor does not hold that view, he or she may be assumed to hold it by members of the congregation. But it is the Church's fault that the very word "immoral" is in the public mind synonymous with sexual irregularity. "Values" has been substituted for the true meaning of the word "morality." This is not an advance.

In Roman Catholic circles the sexual rules have been made for centuries by celibate men. In Protestant circles the rules have been made by happily married men (though their wives were not always consulted to verify this). Most people do not fall in either category. But since the rule makers have long had a tendency to *discuss* mainly with each other while *announcing* to their flock, they are frequently ignorant of people's real lives to the point of irrelevance. When what they preach, formally or informally, does not realistically take account of experience, people are likely to conceal their marital or other sexual difficulties. I have known people to move from one parish to another for this reason, and the original minister never knew why they left. But those are the lucky ones. They at least realized that all clergy are not unapproachable on these subjects. I have known others, under the mistaken impression that clerical opinion was uniform, who abandoned formal religion altogether. Among Protestants that unhappy outcome is most likely from fundamentalist environments but not unknown elsewhere.

Rules versus Principles

The current differences between various factions on the issue of sexuality are extreme. They range from strident insistence, sometimes tinged with panic, on the eternal validity of the strict code of sexual behavior proclaimed in the past (usually including the idea that of all sins the sexual ones are the worst), all the way to equally strident proclamation of extreme permissiveness in the name of Christian love and freedom.

Our religion is full of paradoxes. One which bears most pressingly on our subject is that Christians are urged to adhere to timeless principles ordained by God. But they are simultaneously urged to grow both personally and collectively, to "sing a new song." The Bible is filled with admonitions to discard outworn or childish habits in favor of a better way. Sometimes that better way is in direct violation of what was previously understood to be God's clear commandment. A famous example is Peter's dream, in which he is urged to eat of the animals hitherto forbidden as unclean. And yet, the admonitions to adhere to established traditions are just as frequent.

Few understand the fundamental difference between rules and principles. Principles are eternal, and do not change. Rules do change, since they are only the cultural clothes worn by a principle to suit a particular time and place. For example, in the Old Testament adultery was not only prohibited by the Ten Commandments, but offenders were to be stoned to death. There is, however, considerable evidence that the penalty was seldom invoked. In the New Testament, when the Pharisees were about to stone the woman taken in adultery, Jesus stopped them with the famous words: "Let him who is without sin amongst you cast the first stone." At the same time, he told the woman "Go, and sin no more." Thus he maintained the principle that adultery is wrong but changed the rule about how to deal with offenders.

We are free to change rules, but not to alter basic principles. Mindless adherence to old rules, taking no account of the changed conditions of modern life or of the light shed on the nature of sexuality by psychology and sociology, is not right. It fossilizes tradition instead of preserving it. If we decide to keep some or all of the old rules, it must be because we have established that they express the underlying divine principles in terms which are applicable to contemporary life.

Abolition of all rules is equally likely to be wrong. There is no known culture without some limitations on sexual behavior, and this is nearly always expressed in religious terms. Ours is hardly likely to be the only exception, particularly since our own tradition has always had such limitations. These undoubtedly express some underlying principles, and it is our duty to try to discern what they may be, and to align with them any proposed changes in the rules.

Clergy need to have this distinction firmly in mind and to cultivate the settled habit of considering issues in these terms. Learning to think this way is not easy since all of us tend to confuse the rules we have learned with the principles which ought to govern everyone's behavior. This is particularly true about rules learned in childhood and early youth since these were originally accepted as concrete facts. Many people do not subject them to critical reflection on reaching an age where that is possible. But if this habit is not acquired, it will be very difficult to discern whether secular—or ecclesiastical—changes in the rules are violating religious principles about sexual behavior.[2]

Inadequate Theology of Sex

No coherent theology of sex has been formulated, at least not in a form which reached even most seminarians, let alone the person-in-the-pew. This gap has at least two important causes. First, the sexual tradition of late Christianity differs radically from what is taught in the Old Testament and, as we shall see, from the precepts of early Christianity. Most Christian writers seem unaware of that fact. In addition, neither the physiology nor the psychology of sex was an important focus of scientific inquiry until the last 100 years. Unfortunately many theologians since then have often ignored the results of those investigations. The scientific inquiry itself has often suffered from patriarchal bias, but even so it has produced much reliable information of which theologians ought to be aware. Ignorance of the history of our tradition and of scientific contributions makes thinking through a theology of sex unnecessarily difficult.

What is taught in the Old Testament is dramatically different from the so-called traditional Christian view of sex. In Genesis humankind in the image of God requires both male and female. The word "helpmeet" is more properly translated "partner." The distinction between body and spirit was unknown to the ancient Hebrews and a person was therefore understood to be an indivisible psychophysical unity. In our culture a dualistic view prevails which often clouds understanding of the ancient texts. The true meaning of the verb "to know" as a Biblical term for sexual intercourse is not a euphemism but implies a total experience of the sexual partner at all levels. Sexuality is fundamental to our humanity, one of the energies with which God has endowed us.

This important belief was the basis of the Hebrew objection to neighboring pagan religions. These saw sex as an impersonal divine force which periodically possessed people rather than as an integral part of their humanity. But Judaism never succumbed to the idea that the body is inferior and its passions ought to be rigidly controlled if not eradicated. To this day there are married Christians who believe that they should not make love on Sunday. Some devout Jews, on the contrary, deliberately choose the Sabbath for this purpose to underline the holiness of God's gift of sexuality and to reap its maximum spiritual benefits. Since Christianity began as an offshoot of Judaism, we need to learn how, when, and why its views changed so radically from those of the parent religion.

In a recent article Raymond Lawrence presents some little known facts. He reminds us that the Greco-Roman culture into which Christianity rapidly spread, was infused with a belief in sexual purity. Plato viewed sexual desire as "the diseased aspect of the personality." Body/spirit dualism was a central tenet of philosophy. Lawrence says that "the preserved ecclesiastical documents of the first four centuries of the church's existence reveal clearly the tragic transformation of an essentially Jewish valuation of sexuality into a valuation similar to that of the Neoplatonists and Stoics of the late Greco-Roman world." The earliest documents of the church show minimal interest in sexuality. But sexual asceticism was a prominent feature of the pagan religions, and the early Christians were attacked by Tacitus and Pliny for their lack of sexual purity. Tertullian opposed the Catholics who constituted the mainstream, calling them sensualists. His admiration for pagan asceticism was great because of his own Gnostic tendencies, culminating in his eventual desertion to the Montanists. The idea that Mary and Joseph never had sexual relations and that Mary was a lifelong virgin was not proposed until the 3rd century. As late as the end of the 4th century Christian scholars were objecting to that view on scriptural grounds.

The explanation Lawrence gives for the abandonment of our Jewish roots is cogent. "Whatever else may have hurt their cause, the mainstream Catholic sensualists were radically undermined by the Constantinian adoption of Christianity as the new imperial religion early in the fourth century...With the imperial adoption of the church, idolatry evaporated as a critical issue...Church and empire were one, but as a result the church was in peril of losing its identity. At that juncture...the church seized upon sexual purity, a value already well appreciated by the pagan 'religious' of imperial Rome and various heretical groups, as its new instrument and symbol of identity and control."[3]

Because of their matter/spirit dualism, coupled with the belief that matter was evil and only spirit could be holy, Gnostics had attacked the Incarnation from all sides. They could not believe that Jesus was both fully human and fully divine. The Church managed to fight off the various Gnostic heresies insofar as they threatened the doctrine of the Incarnation, but Gnosticism clung firmly to the skirts of the Church with respect to sex.

This has resulted in some strangely illogical concepts of Christian anthropology and inconsistencies in the doctrine of Creation. On the one hand the body is seen as the temple of the Holy Spirit and bodily resurrection at the Last Day is insisted on. But the body has also been seen as a hotbed of evil passions, particularly in the case of sex, and therefore as something to be at least tamed by the spirit if not transcended entirely. Various combinations of these ideas have been proposed over the centuries. Those holding such views have been oddly unaware of their inherent contradictions. Sin manifests as least as often spiritually as it does physically, as St. Paul frequently pointed out. Not all theologians have made these errors. But the strong if shifting influence of such views is a central reason why our theology of sex has never been truly coherent.

The Reformation offered challenges to this embedded Neoplatonic corruption of the earliest Christian tradition. The abolition of celibacy as a condition for ordination to ministry is the lasting evidence. Luther, who was closer to Jewish roots than Calvin, gave permission for bigamy to Philip of Hesse. And he told a woman with an impotent husband to get his permission to take a lover. Unfortunately Luther never systematized his sexual views so we do not know the theological framework on which he based these decisions.[4]

Over the centuries the dualistic, originally pagan views have been read back into St. Paul by numerous commentators. A recent book by Victor Furnish, *The Moral Teachings of Paul*, makes one wonder how such a misrepresentation of Paul's actual position could ever have occurred. Furnish begins by urging us not to treat Scripture either as a "white elephant" or a "sacred cow." He then explains that contrary to what is often alleged, Paul did not view marriage as an outlet for regrettably ineradicable sexual appetites. "Such an interpretation. . .is explicitly ruled out by his own sharp criticism of 'the heathen' who enter into marriages precisely out of their 'lust.'" Analyzing I Corinthians 7, Furnish concludes that Paul is saying that *"sex must be a shared relationship between two persons of equal standing."*[5]

Thus we see that not only was Paul fighting the dualistic views which have erroneously been retroactively attributed to him, he also did not subscribe to the subordination of women. In discussing I Corinthians 11:2-16, the passage usually quoted in support of patriarchal domination, Furnish is convincing when he says that "Paul's arguments in this passage are *not* addressed to the question of the role or function of women in the church." What is being upheld is that women in church should conform to the prevailing cultural standards of public decency. In a careful analysis of all of Paul's references to women, Furnish documents his view that Paul accepted women as leaders, even teachers, in the church. He draws three conclusions: "1. Paul was committed to the fundamental principle that 'there is neither male nor female' in Christ Jesus. . .2. There is nothing in Paul's concrete teaching on matters pertaining to women that is incompatible with the principle he had affirmed. . . . 3. There is ample evidence that the principle was affirmed by Paul not only in words but in practice."[6] Some readers may have been so conditioned by traditional interpretations that they will be tempted to dismiss Furnish's work. They would do well to remember that there is no barrier to truth so great as the over-familiar word.

Unfortunately the surrounding patriarchal culture, taken together with the pagan dualism about sex, gradually contaminated the idealistic stance of the earliest Christianity. If sex was intrinsically tainted and men superior, how were their sexual urges—so difficult to control—to be explained? Why did prayer, penitence and fasting not eliminate them easily? Blaming women, who were thought inferior anyway, offered an easy way out. Adam tried to offload his responsibility for having eaten the forbidden fruit by saying "the woman tempted me." Patriarchs of the 3rd and subsequent centuries repeated this mistake. Women were the temptresses using the evils of sex to deter men from their proper spiritual development. These views linger on. We can see how formative they have been for our entire culture in the fact that their remnants appear to this day even in those parts of secular society which imagine that they have entirely repudiated religion. Female victims of sexual crimes are blamed—unless they had been "asking for it" they would not have been attacked.

An important psychological factor makes it possible for such unfair practices to persist. One way in which women's sexuality differs from men's is that it actually is easier to divert or control. Religious orders of men have far more difficulty with celibacy than do orders of women. This does not mean that women's sex drive is any weaker than men's. In individual instances the opposite may be the case. But it is very different. The plot of *Lysistrata*, an ancient Greek comedy, depends on the women of Athens and Sparta deciding to stop the war between those cities by withholding sex from their husbands. Nobody could even imagine such a plot with the sexes reversed! Several men have told me that the relative ease with which women control their sex drive is an important factor in men's common, semi-conscious fear of women. Since from the male point of view sex is so overpoweringly strong, men conclude that women must have tremendous hidden power if they are able to control it. When this notion gets coupled with a negative view of sex itself, it is only a short step to the decision that women are to blame for sexual occasions. The equally grave mistake many women have made is to conclude on the basis of men's sexual behavior that they are animals, only after one thing.

Obviously such errors should not be embedded in theology. Here is a place where an intelligent appreciation of the contributions of modern science to the understanding of differences between male and female sexuality can be helpful. If clergy do not avail themselves of these insights as they think through the problems, they run the risk of continuing to cloak unfair prejudices in the precepts of religion. The other risk is that of throwing the baby out with the bathwater—the assumption that because theology has been wrong about some things, it is therefore wrong about everything.

At the present time there are a number of revisionist efforts to modernize the theology of sex. Some of these are also contaminated by the ancient Gnostic error in a subtle way which, if not identified, can be very confusing to those attempting to rethink the issues. The body and its natural urges are glorified, making them determinative for the conduct of sexual life although within the constraint of care for partners. Such views are essentially religion-coated versions of conventional behavioral science wisdom about sex. That science is heavily influenced by 19th century scientific determinism which claims that only matter is real and spirit a foolish illusion. This is just the old Gnostic heresy turned upside down. Once more the intimate, pervasive and indissoluble connection between body and spirit is severed.

Pastoral Problems

Clergy are often caught between compassionate intuitions of how to deal with particular cases and the definite rules they were taught, rules in which at some level they continue to believe. This can be extremely difficult and frustrating. Sometimes it leads to a clerical double life. One inviolable standard is proclaimed from the pulpit in such a way as to suggest that if enough faith and will power to resist temptation is exercised, all can live up to it. But another standard is applied in the pastor's study, with or without conscious reference to situation ethics. This cannot go on very long without being noticed by the congregation, and is often misperceived as hypocrisy. The unfortunate minister may also begin to feel like a hypocrite, and in the worst case a crisis of personal faith ensues.

When this happens, an important distinction has been lost. Upholding whatever the pastor sees as the Christian ideal for the expression of sexuality is a *separate* issue from the question of how to deal pastorally with those who fail one way or another to live up to it. After all, those who fail constitute 100% of everybody. Difficulty in realizing this is a direct consequence of body/spirit dualism taken together with the erroneous view—for which there is no Biblical support whatever—that sexual irregularities are the worst of sins. Violation of the marriage covenant is not simply defined by sleeping in the wrong bed. Cruelty, indifference, demeaning attitudes, riding rough-shod over the partner's needs—all these and many more are also violations of the covenant. Even octogenarians who married their childhood sweethearts, remained virgin until the wedding day and never committed adultery, have all sinned—at least occasionally—in such respects.

Some clergy choose to proclaim an extremely strict standard of sexual conduct and to treat all offenders judgmentally. This does no good. Parishioners may lie to the pastor about what they are really doing, and be hypocritical with one another. Others may develop neurotic symptoms from being overloaded with guilt, and I know of at least two suicides in such cases. Those who have sexual problems for which they truly want pastoral advice may leave the church for another. Some will abandon religion altogether. Newcomers to the community who are divorced or homosexual, who have had an abortion or an illegitimate child, will not come to such a church no matter what other advantages (including doctrinal) it may offer. The congregation is likely to present itself as a society of holy people, thanking God that they are not as others are. But repressed sexuality too often turns septic, and underneath the prim exterior the incidence of spouse abuse, incest and other secret sexual irregularities may be very high. These facts are frequently known to mental health workers in the community as well as to the police or other secular groups. Their respect for religion is destroyed.

Pastors who go to the other extreme hardly fare better. I have seen cases where people who went for marriage counseling with a range of difficulties including some sexual issues were given half-digested snippets of sex education, including instruction in how to masturbate so that they could learn "to enjoy their God-given bodies." The emotional and spiritual aspects of their trouble were underplayed or ignored altogether. I have also known two homosexual men whose pastors told them in their youth that they should "accept the sexuality God gave them." After years of trying to do that, they finally dealt with their homosexuality by other means (one through therapy, one through religious counseling) and married happily. But now they were too old to start families, and deeply resented the bad advice they got from their pastors years before. Even the American Psychiatric Association acknowledges that if homosexuality is experienced as undesirable, the person may seek help in overcoming it.

Clergy who do things like this are horrified by the other pastoral extreme, and strive to promote a climate of acceptance for all in a spirit of Christian love. But both groups are making essentially the same mistake. They are so carried away by a particular ideology that they do not attend to the real needs of individuals in their care. In both cases, people come asking for the bread of help and forgiveness but are given a stone instead. One is the stone of condemnation. The other is the stone of denying the problem.

The Christian ideal for sexuality as the pastor understands it, no matter how strict that may be, should be presented *only as an ideal* from which all depart. All ways of departing from it should be given equal weight, not singling out the way of genital action for special condemnation. In fact, if less tangible violations are appropriately dealt with, the genital ways sometimes disappear by themselves. For instance, couples in a faithful relation of trusting intimacy are not likely to commit adultery. Therefore prompt and competent attention to cases of marital incompatibility should be seen as part of the pastoral task of upholding the sexual standard. All ways of departing from the ideal demonstrate a need for help and forgiveness, and the pastor must urgently refrain from being either accusatory or superficial when problems are brought to his or her attention. In some cases professional counseling will be recommended, but this will always be an adjunct to confession and reconciliation.

The task of continuing to hold up the ideal as a goal toward which all should work as best they can, while offering compassionate help to those who fail, will be far easier if it is never forgotten that the only way anyone (including the pastor) can stand before God is as a forgiven sinner.

NOTES—CHAPTER II

1. Susan Hanks, op.cit. in Chapter I
2. Ruth Tiffany Barnhouse, "Is There a Divine Intention for the Man/Woman Relationship?" In Sexual Archetypes, ed. Bina Gupta. (To be published January 1987 by Paragon Press).
3. Raymond J. Lawrence, "The Church and the Sexual Revolution," Quarterly Review (Spring 1985,Vol.5, No.1).
4. Luther's Works, vol. 36, Word and Sacrament II, eds.: Abdel R. Wentz & Helmut T. Lehmann, (Fortress Press, 1959, p.103).
5. Victor Furnish, The Moral Teaching of Paul, (Nashville: Abingdon, 1979, p.35), emphasis in original.
6. ibid., p.111.

CHAPTER III

Personal Problems for Clergy

Problems are not the same for clergy who reached maturity before the sexual revolution as for those reaching it during or after the late 1960s. This is because many attitudes to sexuality are formed before the age of seven even though they are not articulated until much later. Modifications occur during adolescence, depending on what factors in family, culture and church the young person is exposed to. By the end of adolescence sexual ideals and beliefs about sexual morality are definitely molded. Therefore, the sudden shift in the '60s makes the formation of older and younger groups radically different. This is not to say that adults cannot alter their views, but it does describe the starting point which is likely to be adhered to in the absence of compelling reasons for change. Inconsistency may also be found in those who have changed some but not all of the beliefs absorbed in childhood and early youth. But in spite of the generalizations I am about to make, I earnestly caution against stereotyping on the basis of age. In individual cases these generalizations may be wrong, for better or worse.

Differences in Attitude to Others

In dealing with others, members of each group have the built-in advantages and disadvantages of their particular formation. We all know clergy who are legalistic, prudish, uncompromising and essentially unforgiving to those who engage in various sexual irregularities. Such ministers are more likely to be found in the group that came to maturity prior to the revolution.

On the other hand, members of this group are more likely to realize that sexual standards are necessary for the integrity of the social fabric, and for the preservation of the family as the basic unit of society. They are unlikely to make the error of confusing freedom with mere license. They are also likely to avoid putting undue stress on the value of immediate gratification, recognizing that in the service of distant goals—perhaps even eternal goals—gratification will often at least need to be postponed, and in some cases forsworn altogether.

Many clergy who came to maturity after the revolution have been raised to think that guilt is a dirty word. They do not realize that it is a valuable, built-in faculty of the human psyche. It is a sign that something is wrong. It bears the same relation to the psyche as fever does to the body. A doctor who thought that all fever should be immediately abolished with antipyretic drugs without first finding out its cause would quickly be recognized as a dangerous fool. Fever only tells us that we are sick without telling us whether the underlying disorder is trivial or serious. Guilt functions in precisely the same way. It is true that much guilt is neurotic—trivial in terms of its cause. This is the kind of guilt psychiatrists see a good deal of, and may account for their general attitude that the thing to do with guilt is get rid of it. But just as people whose temperature regulation mechanism is disturbed may be critically ill before knowing anything is wrong, simply because they did not run a fever in the early stages, so there are many people who do not feel guilt when they should. They are spiritually sick without knowing it. The Nuremberg Trials at the close of World War II were the attempt of an outraged civilization to deal with such people.

Young clergy are more likely than their elders to trivialize guilt. Such clergy forget that Christian forgiveness is meaningless when guilt is unacknowledged. Nor do they realize that many of their flock, upon whom they have too quickly pressed forgiveness, continue to feel the guilt they brought to the pastor. It simply festers in their psyche. Some now have two things to feel guilty about instead of one—the original difficulty and the fact that they cannot accept what the minister said about it. Psychiatrists know that it is often guilt which paradoxically leads people to further mistakes. Ministers who offer hasty forgiveness are sometimes baffled by such results. It is well to remember that no two consciences are exactly alike. When people come for advice about some sexual irregularity, the pastor should not immediately judge it by his or her own standards and advise accordingly. Instead, a painstaking inquiry into the parishioner's own sexual value system is called for. That should not, of course, be the only basis on which advice is finally given, but if it is ignored, the advice is more than likely to be bad.

Finally, younger clergy who trivialize guilt in this way are far more likely than their elders to include men and women who succumb (either in their own case or that of others) to the lure of instinctual self-indulgence dressed up in the language of liberation.

The younger group do, however, have some important advantages over their elders. The church is currently involved in making the valuable transition from treating sexual offenses juridically to treating them penitentially. This has always been the custom in the Orthodox branches of Christianity, and there it has saved a good deal of the trouble Western Christians are now going through. Young clergy are likely to welcome this transition and to make it easily, while it may make some of their elders nervous.

Dealing with youth, many of whom were not born until after the sexual revolution and whose parents may have been among its standard bearers, can be extremely baffling. Younger clergy are more likely than their elders to understand what is going on, and to find ways of teaching Christian principles which do not sound ante-diluvian to the space-age, TV-conditioned youth.

The differences can also cause serious communication problems as clergy of different age-groups relate to one another. Young pastors should remember that clergy in the higher levels of their judicatories nearly always belong to the older group, to those least likely to understand or accept any part of the sexual revolution. And those higher up on the ecclesiastical ladder should remember that the young pastors had dramatically different formation than their own. Even when they agree with their elders about some standard, they are likely to give very different reasons, or at least to express their reasons in different language.

I know a bishop in his sixties who once addressed a group of younger clergy on the subject of premarital chastity. He said he had had no trouble with it as a young man, he and his wife had had a happy relationship, and he therefore saw no reason why everybody couldn't do likewise. End of discussion. The reaction of his hearers was "there goes the bishop again"—and they promptly all went out and did their own thing, whatever that was. The bishop himself thought he had been impressively heard. I know that he had many valuable pastoral insights which could have helped the young ministers in his charge, but after that introduction they were unable to listen to him.

It *is* possible to expound traditional ideals in terms which the young can understand, but that's not the way to go about it. It is tempting for many older clergy to rely on a "Thus saith the Lord!" approach without informing themselves about what is actually going on, or appreciating what evils the sexual revolution was intended to correct. They also have often not informed themselves about the contribution of the behavioral sciences to the understanding of sexuality. Nor have they read some of the very thoughtful work being done by church historians and theologians attempting to grapple with the problems. Some even make traditional sexual views the acid test of orthodoxy in general. If they persist in these errors, they will not be heard, nor will they understand the unrest in those under their jurisdiction.

Younger clergy who need to discuss some sexual matter with older authorities would do well to bear all these differences in mind. The first task is to communicate effectively that the traditional position is not just being ignored. If the young minister is sexually avant-garde, he or she would be wise to begin with some evidence of orthodoxy about other issues. It should also be clarified that the traditional position is understood and taken seriously, even if not agreed with in whole or in part. Disagreement should be introduced with evidence of having thought the issue through theologically, not just in contemporary secular terms. In short, homework must be done.

If both groups could bear constantly in mind the possible differences in outlook, communication between them would be greatly improved. And that would benefit not only the clergy but also the whole Church.

Problems in Private Life

Since sexuality is a powerful component of everyone's humanity, and since there is no person immune from its influence, the factors discussed above will also affect the private life of clergy. They may combine with other serious issues to lay traps for the unwary.

All sexual attitudes and behavior have social consequences. The basic forms of social exchange are sex, money, power and language. These have traditionally been the focus of social ethics, whether Christian or secular. But, as Philip Turner points out, "...there are voices both within the church and in society as a whole that are making an unprecedented demand—that sexual relations as such be singled out from all others and removed from the subject matter of social ethics altogether...it is argued that society ought to stay out of the bedroom....Sex is a personal and not a social matter."[1]

The only sexual act which might be thought entirely personal is masturbation. But people masturbate for a variety of reasons, all of which are ultimately social. If they prefer themselves to all others, they are rejecting others—a social decision. If they masturbate in order to remain sexually faithful to an absent or incapacitated spouse, that decision is based on the marital relationship and is therefore also social. Any other motive, when analyzed, will be seen to have social dimensions.

Sexual acts involving other people are clearly social. Decisions to abstain from sex or not to marry are also social since they reduce the number of people in the pool of available mates. Decisions about how many children to have are very obviously social. In China, where population control to avoid general poverty and famine twenty years from now is a high priority, people are forbidden by law to have more than one child. Americans socialized to think of sexual decisions as completely private and personal are horrified by this, seeing only an assault on personal freedom. They are blind to the social consequences of sexual behavior. How they can think this way in the face of such domestic problems as the high rate of pregnancy in unmarried teenagers is hard to fathom.

Even sexual attitudes are social. Ask any woman subject to verbal sexual harassment at work or school. The social life of her mother or grandmother was completely different, since in those days men believed that sexual conversation with ladies, or even in their presence, was uncouth.

I have made this point at length so that clergy will not be taken in by the cry, "But it doesn't affect anybody but us!" whether they hear that in their study or in their own head as they wrestle with a personal situation. Nothing but bad decisions can come of ignoring the social dimension of sexuality. The point is easier to keep in mind if one avoids the culture's dualistic view that sex is merely recreational, like going skiing, only more fun and less expensive. Sex is far more than recreation, although that aspect is undeniable. As we saw in the last chapter, the emotional and spiritual aspects are very important, especially to women.

There is another problem with the current truncated view of sex. Only immediate consequences tend to be considered, especially when feeling is running strong. The probability of self-deception in such situations is very high. Paradoxically, this probability is higher with clergy than in the general population. They have been taught that sex is meaningful at many levels and genuinely wish to take the feelings of their partners into account. This may lead them to cloak a doubtful sexual liaison with pseudo-spiritual double-talk. An anguished clergyman caught in the aftermath of such a situation once said to me "But we prayed about it together first—what could have gone wrong?"

This kind of thing can be avoided most of the time if the full *social* ramifications of a possible sexual encounter, not only in the present but into the future, are considered carefully beforehand. This includes a realistic appraisal of the actual life situation (including the psychology) of the other person. Nor must the differences between male and female sexuality be forgotten.

Male clergy need to realize that a woman's "consent" is not enough. Congregations abound with lonely women, both married and single. Many of these will at least yield to, if not actually solicit, sexual attentions from clergy in order to get some companionship. Some behave this way because the culture has trained them to believe it is the only way to get serious attention from men. Others do so out of a naive belief that *other* men might take advantage of them but clergy certainly would not. It should be realized that it is impossible, even with the best will in the world, *not* to take advantage of women who are sexually compliant for such reasons. I address this advice to male clergy because I have never heard of a woman minister making this particular mistake, though I suppose it is not actually impossible.

Clergy would also do well to remember that they live in a goldfish bowl. I have known many who confidently assumed that various aspects of their private life were unknown to anyone but themselves. In fact, I had already heard everything they had to tell me, luridly embroidered, from members of their congregation. Not a few clergy have been so indiscreet that removal from their pastorate was necessary to deal with the scandal. Some of those have not learned their lesson, and take no reponsibility for what happened. They only complain about what they call the narrow-minded bigotry of those responsible for their downfall. Whether or not actual bigotry played a part, they should recognize that what happened to them is definite proof of the social dimension of sex.

Some women clergy naively but sincerely assume that their status, especially when wearing a clerical collar, is an automatic protection against sexual advances. The consequences of this mistake range from minor embarrassment to real danger. I know of a woman minister who was raped by a man who phoned saying he was in great spiritual distress and needed to see her immediately. She foolishly met him after hours in the deserted church. More often women clergy are the target of unexpected sexual advances, even from members of their congregation or from fellow clergy. The cause is the women's illusory sense of invulnerability to such occasions. For instance, at a clergy conference they may have accepted an invitation to meet a male colleague in his hotel room "to discuss tomorrow's agenda." Before entering the ministry these women would automatically have known enough to suggest a different location.

A few women use the "protection" of their clergy status as a screen behind which they engage in overtly seductive behavior. Men taking this at face value are in for a rude surprise since these women respond with outrage and may even make real trouble for them. Such cases are very difficult to evaluate, since the woman is usually not conscious of her motives and has deceived herself as well as the men involved. Any woman minister who has had such trouble with men more than once should ask herself what she might be doing to provoke it. One mistake may be genuine naivete, but only one. Of course this does not excuse the men's behavior but, unless drunk or bent on violence, men rarely make *serious* passes at women who have not—if only unwittingly—sent some signal of receptivity.

Since clergy have little or no control over what part of a city they must visit, often having to go after dark, women need to be realistic about their vulnerability. They should consider taking a course in methods of self-defense provided by most police departments, and older women should not assume that they are no longer at risk. They also need to know that there are perverse men who take special pleasure in sexual harassment (or worse) of women clergy and nuns. The collar is no substitute for practical methods of self-protection.

Another common problem is that of male clergy committing adultery. This is frequently a sign of vocational confusion, complicated or caused by stress and burnout. We all know that clergy are shamefully overworked, often putting in 80-hour weeks. They are also grossly underpaid and often under-appreciated. Janet Fishburn says that "although male clergy experience doubts about vocation and marriage similar to those of other men, the present situation of the church and ministry may intensify the midlife crisis for clergymen. . .As has been observed in life-cycle literature, an affair is a common response to midlife crisis."[2]

The clergyman may see the woman involved as a gift of God to relieve his misery. This is *never* true. She is actually being *used* to put off the necessity of squarely facing the real problem. Occasionally the parties to such an adulterous affair are not just deceiving themselves but truly love one another. The marriage which is being injured has long been seen as a miserable mistake. Unfortunately, the social consequences of an affair may ruin the new love as well as break up the old marriage, and the effect on the minister's congregation may be disastrous.

Other kinds of male clergy adultery inspire much less sympathy. I have known men who see their congregation as a happy hunting ground for indulging their sexual appetites, counting on people's unwillingness to think ill of clergy to protect them from exposure. Most judicatories deal far too leniently with such men when the situation finally becomes untenable. A transfer is often the worst the culprits have to face, and they may start up all over again in the new place. I see this as the old-boy custom of covering up for one another, and I see it as despicable. Just because it happens in the church does not prevent it from being one of the signs of decadent patriarchy. The usual excuse—"let's keep this quiet to avoid scandal"—does not fool the victims.

Clergy of both sexes must not assume that deep friendship or spiritual companionship automatically imply sexual attraction. The issue often surfaces between clergy working together, or with a member of the congregation or lay staff. One difficulty is that American culture tends to prematurely or altogether inappropriately sexualize practically everything. This puzzles many foreigners who often see us as really deranged on the subject of sex. It seems to be impossible to sell anything without draping a sexually provocative woman across it. Less obvious (but equally weird) is a typical TV commercial showing a woman apparently having an orgasm at the sight of a newly waxed kitchen floor! Most of us are so used to such things that we don't realize how odd they are or what effect such constant exposure to sex has had on our own attitudes. Any closeness, let alone real intimacy, is assumed to have a sexual base.

Both men and women pastors have consulted me about their fears of sexual involvement with a valued co-worker, or they may be worried about the advisability of hiring such a person. When I ask whether they actually feel any sexual attraction, they frequently say no—and sometimes go on to wonder what is wrong with them that they don't! I have to explain the nature of friendship, about which they may know little or nothing.

In some of these cases sexual attraction does develop when marriage cannot be considered, and those involved sometimes feel helpless to do anything but give in. This is more likely in younger people who may have little or no experience in denying strong sexual attraction. Even if they have not acted on such feelings in the past, there is so much talk in the surrounding culture urging sexual fulfillment, and so few voices raised suggesting continence, that the temptation to rationalize a decision to proceed may be extremely strong. This is especially likely for those who are unhappily married. But since deep friendship is the primary base of the tempting relationship, each party should have the long-range good of the other in mind. An affair, however gratifying in the short run, is more than likely to lead to future pain. It should be remembered that the sexual element is only one strand in the fabric of such relationships, and that continence is not only possible but can be very rewarding. When people finally realize that they have sex, it doesn't have them, the resulting sense of being in control of one's life rather than at its mercy brings great freedom.

There is a great vogue at present for "free, honest and open communication." On the whole, this is a good thing. However, some people mistakenly interpret it to mean that they must reveal their feelings, especially to those concerned. To do otherwise feels hypocritical. Such a view fails to note the difference between hypocrisy and discretion. Some things really are better left unsaid.

Sexual feelings toward another person which ought not to be acted on should not be revealed, much less discussed. The other person may not reciprocate those feelings, and nothing but awkwardness in the relationship can result from communicating them. There may have been a pleasant atmosphere of easy comradeship, perhaps including an occasional hug, taking meals together and so forth, which will be spoiled by a unilateral sexual revelation. The one who does not have such feelings is likely to withdraw emotionally for fear of deceptive encouragement of the other. This can only be experienced as a painful rejection. Nevertheless, that withdrawal is really necessary since continuing on the old basis is far too likely to stir false hopes in the romantically afflicted person. Worse still are cases like that of a woman assistant pastor who made the mistake of telling her boss how she felt about him. The result was that he led her on with meaningless "sweet talk" while getting her to do far more than her share of the parish work.

If there is any possibility that the feelings are mutual, it is even more important not to talk about them. We often make the mistake of thinking that words are only words and do not lead to action. In fact, we believe that talk about some things serves the valuable function of clearing the air. This is true in some situations, but it is definitely not true in sexual ones. Sexual talk is in itself sexually stimulating. Far from defusing the tricky situation, talk about sexual feelings may cause them to burst into flame. Any chance of keeping the relationship on the desired plane of friendship is thereby destroyed.

Family Problems

Married clergy are unlikely to get seriously embroiled in any of the problems discussed above if their family life is in order. The best prevention is to spend real time cultivating the relationship with one's own spouse. Clergy negotiating contracts with a parish should insist on regular time off, not to be intruded on except in the direst of emergencies. There are very few crises which cannot wait at least twelve hours. Many clergy spouses have reason to fear that the time allotted to them is the lowest priority, likely to be set aside every time Mrs. Weepalot phones that she must see the pastor "right now!" or Mr. Bigshot insists that this is the only time he has free to discuss repairs to the church roof.

Spouses and children who are neglected in this way often resort to a variety of negative methods to get the absent parent's attention. Home becomes an unpleasant place to be. The already overworked minister may take refuge in still more church activity, and a vicious circle of mutually destructive behavior is set up. The pastor's home life is then no sort of model for families in the congregation, and his or her ability to provide wise counsel to those in trouble is called into question.

Above all, clergy must resist the temptation to deny or cover up family problems in order to preserve their image in the community. People in all walks of life think up ingenious reasons for not facing problems and getting necessary help in dealing with them. Those are rationalizations, and most clergy have experience in persuading members of their congregations to give up such foolish delaying tactics. In my experience, clergy themselves are the worst offenders. For example, I have known pastors who refused to join AA, or to let family members join, in order to prevent anybody outside the family from knowing there was a problem. This is asking for even worse trouble, and in any case others are not blind. How can parishioners be persuaded to accept help if the one advising them will not?

Dr. Jerry Lewis has written a wonderful book called *How's Your Family?* in which he explains in nontechnical terms just what goes into the development of healthy families. The foundation is a marital relationship characterized by shared power and real intimacy. Intimacy is beautifully defined as "the mutual exchange of private worlds." Children know that the parents are in charge, but they also know that they will be carefully listened to and their feelings taken into account in family decisions.[3] All this takes time, real time, consistent time. Without such investment of time there can be no real happiness or comfort. In the long run it does not take nearly as much time as dealing with divorce, disturbed children, distraught congregations and disapproving superiors. When ministers recognize that modeling a healthy family is really part of their Christian vocation, it becomes much easier to set aside the necessary time and to train co-workers and congregations to respect it.

Divorce

But what if the best, most conscientious efforts do not work? What if divorce really cannot be avoided? The most traditional view is that divorce can always be avoided, but those who take that position do not think about the price which must be paid in human misery. Usually both—but at least one—of the partners must endure a level of personal unhappiness, of denial of real needs, which would not be demanded in any other circumstances. Children are presented with a dreadful model of marriage and home life which adversely affects their development in many ways. I have had many more patients whose parents did not get divorced when they should have than patients traumatized by a broken home. The old view that once a marriage was sexually consummated it was indissoluble has been abandoned even by the Roman Catholic church. Now it is understood that consummation must take place on mental, emotional and spiritual levels for there to be a true marriage. Unfortunately, this does not always happen. Sometimes, and this is frequent among clergy, the couple tries for years to effect the necessary unions before they finally give up.

Church officials holding to the older view often fail to pay attention to marital problems among the clergy under their care. They may make it extremely difficult for ministers to consult them on such issues and absolutely impossible for spouses. If they are approached at all, they just tell the sufferer to go home, bite the bullet and be a good Christian. At the same time they wonder what the younger clergy are coming to, with all that dreadful divorce, never realizing that their own mishandling of such situations may be part of the cause.

A more truly Christian attitude is expressed by the Paulist priest James Young, who founded the Conference of Separated and Divorced Catholics. In an inspiring book, the fruit of over ten years of work with thousands of deeply religious people tragically caught in the problems of divorce, he says that "some marriage relationships become over time loveless and even destructive. To remain in a commitment which is bringing harm and continuing stress at the risk of everyone's well-being is not fidelity; it may be fear. The decision to divorce and end a loveless, empty relationship may be a courageous act of fidelity to God. God, who is ever faithful to us, calls us to grow through even the death of a marriage commitment to find a new committed life."[4] He adds that wise consideration of divorce calls for a creative tension between the value of permanence and the value of compassion. The Bible teaches both values. One cannot simply adopt a theory of divorce which abandons either value in favor of the other without making serious mistakes.

I cannot emphasize too strongly that early, informed attention to the slightest marital complaint, with easy referral to professional counselors if necessary, could avert many divorces. If problems go undealt with for too long, resentments build up, unforgettable hurts are inflicted and the rift becomes so deep that it cannot be healed.

In a book provocatively titled *The Five Divorces of a Healthy Marriage*, Harold Straughn describes the value of real attention to marital problems before they get out of hand in these words: "The momentum of marriage is sometimes interrupted. Periods of disequilibrium halt seasons of equilibrium. Then a new stage of harmony and balance sets in, better than anything you'd experienced before. Sometimes the interruptions are so serious that people think the relationship is at an end, especially when they're unaware of what's happening. And sometimes the relationship dies because no one knew how to deal with the transition."[5]

Nothing is ever gained by putting one's head in the sand and hoping a marital problem will just go away. Church authorities who refuse to deal adequately with requests for help are cruelly irresponsible and actually undermine their own standards. After listing friendship, work, parenting, patriotism and many other kinds of relationship, Straughn says that they all depend on marriage as the basic form of human connectedness. He knows that marriage is the microcosm of society, the matrix in which all social relationships are born and must be nourished if they are to succeed. It is therefore worth the very closest attention.

When all attempts to heal a problematic marriage have been unsuccessful, divorce is inevitable. Many people do not know that divorce is like everything else: there is a right and a wrong way to go about it. Clergy have a strong obligation to do it right. The goal of the right way is to minimize the mess. Details may vary from case to case, but there are some general rules.

First, do not even *think* about starting any new relationship before divorce is final. New partners chosen on the rebound are likely to be wrong. Until one really knows why the marriage failed, one is all too likely to make the same mistake all over again. That is stupidly unfair, not only to oneself but to the prospective new mate. It also builds up unnecessary resentment in the former spouse, confuses the children and risks public scandal. Even after a divorce is complete, those who manage to select the right new mate in less than two years are just lucky. It takes time for wounds to heal.

This points to the second rule, which is that some counseling is essential. Many couples stop going to the marriage counselor when the decision to divorce is made. That is wrong. There needs to be real communication about the true nature of the failure, and this is often impossible until the irrevocability of that failure is acknowledged. Both partners must come to understand their own contribution to the breakup, not just the other's faults. If they do not, there is only a legal divorce, the couple remaining negatively bound together. The inevitable feelings of guilt and hostility must be faced and thoroughly worked through. If that painful process is bypassed, those unfinished feelings are likely to be acted out in the lawyer's office in the form of bitter wrangling over property and child custody. What is worse, the fight may continue long after the divorce, with the children caught in the middle.

A custom which has much to recommend it is growing in a number of denominations. At the time of the divorce, the couple—possibly accompanied by their children—go through a penitential service of reconciliation. They ask forgiveness of each other and of God, and pray for grace that their unhappy experience may not damage their trust or their ability to love.

Divorced clergy, especially if remarried, may have problems lay people generally do not face. They must remember that the sexual revolution is not equally advanced everywhere. There are strong regional differences not only about the acceptability of divorce itself, but also about what is expected of clergy as distinct from laity. Ecclesiastical authorities often handle the embarrassing problem of placing divorced clergy by sending them far away. Those in charge of the new jurisdiction may be personally quite liberal, and have an announced policy of accepting clergy who are divorced or in a second marriage. They then confidently assume that their policies will be implemented by congregations in their jurisdiction. Such confidence is often badly misplaced.

I know of a divorced pastor who moved from the northeast to a large, sophisticated city in the southwest with his new wife. She found an excellent job in her field immediately, and church authorities assured him that he would have no trouble. He applied to several parishes and was always on the short list but never chosen. His self-confidence was undermined, and he sought counseling since his depression was adversely affecting the new marriage. The counselor was aware of the deep conservatism of the church in that city, on which the liberal views of the recently elected authorities had not yet made any significant impression. The clergyman discovered that his place on short lists was in deference to the announced policy of the judicatory, but that no parish had any intention of hiring him in spite of his excellent credentials and past record of success. On the advice of the counselor, the couple returned north. This painful drama took over a year, and the wife's professional career was seriously interrupted.

Such examples show that it can be unwise to rely on church officials for accurate information about true conditions in the prospective new location. Clergy contemplating such a move should do their own investigating, questioning both other ministers and laity. If the committee interviewing the prospective candidate does not raise the issue of the divorce, the interviewee should do so.

Special Problems Facing Homosexual Clergy

If there is prejudice against divorce in many places, the prejudice against homosexuality is even deeper and more widespread. Clergy known to be homosexual have all the practical problems of divorced clergy and then some. Those whose homosexuality is not known have other problems, including fear of the consequences of discovery and moral anxiety about concealing their orientation, to name just two. There is no question that homosexual persons are still severely scapegoated in many parts of society, and this is often worst in the church. They may be automatically suspected of seducing young people and molesting children, in spite of the fact that such offenses are rare in homosexuals and common in heterosexuals. To be constantly assaulted by such prejudice, whether one's own orientation is open or concealed, is degrading and humiliating.

I can understand the temptation to lump all that together under the general rubric of fascist oppression. It is then only a short step to the conclusion that any questioning of the normality of homosexuality stems from such ugly attitudes. However, I am convinced that this way of viewing things is not only untrue but counterproductive for homosexuals themselves.

The point made earlier that *all sexual decisions are social* is relevant here. Those who proclaim a sexual standard different from that generally accepted must be prepared for serious debate. It is not really difficult to discriminate between those who object on the basis of hostile prejudice and those whose questions stem from serious thought about theological or other principles. There is no point in discussion with hysterical stone throwers, whether the issue is homosexuality, racism, or anything else. But those who are earnestly grappling with the issues deserve a serious, undefensive response.

Not only that, but such a response is in the best practical interest of homosexual clergy. It will be more likely than defensiveness (much less anger!) to secure the sympathetic support of church officials, and will sometimes work even when those officials have serious doubts in principle about homosexuality. And homosexual clergy, even more than those with divorce or other problems, really need the support of authorities. If this is unobtainable, a move to a more sympathetic jurisdiction should be considered.

This chapter has tried to deal with practical problems, isolated, so far as possible, from theoretical positions. Some suggestions about theologically based standards for acceptable sexual behavior, whether homosexual or heterosexual, will be discussed in the next chapter.

NOTES—CHAPTER III

1. Philip Turner, *Sex, Money & Power*, (Cambridge, MA: Cowley Publications, 1985, p.30.

2. Janet Fishburn, "Male Clergy Adultery as Vocational Confusion," *The Christian Century*, September 15-22, 1982.

3. The deplorable tendency to sweep the sexual irregularities of clergy under the rug is illustrated by the fact that when this excellent and illuminating article was printed, the editor was severely criticized for having brought this touchy subject into the open.

3. Jerry M. Lewis, M.D., *How's Your Family?* (New York: Brunner/Mazel, Inc., 1979. Based on research into family systems, this highly recommended book is written for the general public. It contains helpful questionnaires to assist readers in assessing the relationships in their own families. The book should be in the library of every clergyperson as an invaluable aid in counseling.

4. James J. Young, C.S.P., *Divorcing, Believing, Belonging*, (Ramsey, NJ: The Paulist Press, 1984, p. 149). This is another book all clergy should read. It is also one which can be given to parishioners. The section on Roman marriage law is easily skipped, and the rest of the book should be applicable to all Christians.

5. Harold Straughn, *The Five Divorces of a Healthy Marriage*, (St. Louis: CBP Press, 1986). This book applies stage theory to the development of marriage. The popular style makes it accessible to everyone, not just clergy or other marriage counselors—all of whom should own it.

CHAPTER IV

About a Theology of Sex

The influence of patriarchy on the negative aspects of the current sexual revolution was discussed in Chapter I, but this basic feature of human social organization has had other effects as well. In considering modification of sexual customs it is important to dissect out the influence of patriarchy as such. The enduring principles we all wish to protect would obviously be expressed in different rules under that system than in the post-patriarchal era toward which we are now groping. The close reasoning which the dissection requires is not easy, since nobody can possibly have the necessary objectivity. We are all sexual, and we have all been conditioned by patriarchy. Only with difficulty can we bring a significant amount of that conditioning to awareness, and much is doomed to remain unconscious.

It is impossible to detach ourselves from these facts, to view the social change in which we are all caught up with the disinterested impartiality of, say, an anthropologist from outer space. All anyone can do is to contribute to the discussion, trusting that two or three hundred years from now, after many views have been examined and tested, our species will have improved rather than worsened its state. But this lays a great responsibility on all who speak to these issues. We cannot use the current uncertainty about standards as an opportunity to dress up our own inclinations or prejudices in fancy theoretical language, thus enabling ourselves to do as we please while ignoring our obligation to the larger discussion. Both honesty and humility are highly desirable in anyone venturing to do theology, but when it comes to sexual theology, they are essential.

At the same time, nobody is likely to tackle this subject without having developed a position which they find convincing, one which will at least differ from, if not actually be opposed to, other positions. I am no exception. My own view will shine through my attempts to present other views as fairly as I can. I hope readers will remember that I see myself as only one contributor to an important discussion, the eventual outcome of which probably none of us will live to see.

Body/Spirit Issues

A workable theology of sex must begin by considering factors which are not obviously sexual. Focusing on sexual acts is a mistake which has been made by both secular and religious theorists. The errors of modern sexologists were discussed in Chapter II. Much the same errors characterize the old lists of sexual sins, which ranked all sexual acts in order of their moral deplorability. Contemporary behavioral science and old-fashioned theology both concentrate on bodily behavior, social and relational issues being considered peripherally if at all. Both minimize or, in some cases, actually deny the indissoluble connection between body and spirit. The fact that one system glorifies and the other vilifies the acts in question is irrelevant to this point.

Nearly all branches of the church have recognized that the old ways of dealing with sexual matters are no longer workable. Philip Turner (Professor of Ethics at General Theological Seminary) says that there are currently three basic types of revisionist sexual ethics, and he calls these libertarian, self-actualizationist, and personalist. He says "libertarians hold that, with the exception of the duty to prevent the birth of unwanted children, there is no need for ethics to make any specific proposals about sexual behavior as such."[1]

Self-actualizationists believe that sexual encounters should contribute to human development. "No form of sexual behavior, however, is wrong in itself. It is wrong *only* insofar as it impedes growth or injures health."[2] Turner doubts that either of these positions will carry the day since both can be (and have been) used to justify such generally abhorrent practices as sado-masochism, impersonal promiscuity, incest, and sexual acts committed with children. Both construe sexual relations primarily as private contracts. Such relativization of sexual codes ignores the inescapable social ramifications of all sexual behavior, and therefore does not see that to construe sex as only serving the needs or wishes of individuals involved in particular acts is narcissistically antisocial. Narcissism and selfishness are indistinguishable in practice, so here is a noticeable convergence of pathology and sin.

From the theological point of view, these positions are just the other side of the old religious coin since they focus on sexual acts, with little or no attention to the psychodynamics even of the participants. To be sure, conscious wishes, unless immediately and obviously destructive, may be indulged. But we now know how often conscious impulses conceal unconscious processes which may be quite different. Transpersonal considerations, such as the spiritual or symbolic significance of sexual behavior, are simply ignored.

The personalist position, however, is more attractive and has many adherents. It relies very heavily on the primacy of *personhood*, which is understood to be antecedent to, and somehow separate from, our identity as *men* or *women*, or as members of any particular group. Personhood emphasizes and values individuality over the values of community. It argues powerfully against stereotyping or discrimination on the basis of sex, race, social class or anything else—including sexual preferences.

In view of the church's sad record of just such unchristian discrimination, an anthropology which rules that out has much to be said for it. Personalism is strongly relational and emphasizes not only the rights of individuals but also their duties and obligations to others. Turner says that "the communal and relational overtones of personalist images sound closer to traditional Christian values and perceptions than do the more economic and self-referential ones with which they contend."[3]

Unfortunately, the technique personalism uses to accomplish its ends is fundamentally dualist. "They split human nature between an inner reality they call the *person* and an outer container or instrument they call the *body*."[4] Sexuality is ascribed to personhood and has no integral connection with the body, which becomes merely the tool which a *person* uses to express his or her unique configuration of sexuality. It is on the basis of this split that personalists argue for homosexuality, some kinds of adultery, and sexual relations between single people. These are acceptable, provided that the highest values of one's own and the partner's *personhood* are being expressed.

If the church has erred in the past by construing fidelity as *only* physical, then personalism errs in the other direction by construing it as *everything but* physical. I do not see how dualism can avoid falling into one or another of these errors. Theological reasons for rejecting dualism were set out in Chapter II, and psychosomatic medicine provides modern scientific reasons. It demonstrates the indissoluble connection between body and psyche, whether psyche is understood as personhoood, spirit, soul, or any combination thereof.[5] The point can be made even more simply. Remember the last time you awoke with a nightmare, with heart pounding and a catch in your breath. Vividly recall any emotionally powerful experience from your past, and note the immediate change in your bodily sensations, which will be similar to those accompanying the original event, though perhaps not quite as strong.

Patriarchy

Many valuable elements of human social organization were developed during the patriarchal period, and these need to be maintained. They include practically everything that we associate with civilization itself. At issue are only those features of patriarchy which prevent us from living out the ideal of Gal.3:28. Their influence is often very subtle. The idea of male supremacy is in the very air we all breathe from infancy, men and women alike. Mere intellectual repudiation of it is not enough to banish its effects.[6]

We saw earlier that men are first interested in the physical aspects of sex, and it is not uncommon for a man's sexual urges (as distinct from his sexual commitments, if any) to remain more or less independent of his relationships, nor does this fact mean that there is necessarily anything wrong with him. This is not true of women, and even in this permissive era they do not reach the peak of sexual responsiveness until their thirties or later. Women never lose the preference for sexual encounters occurring in the context of a satisfying relationship. Many women, even those reaching maturity in the last twenty years, and with no anti-sexual childhood conditioning, have told me that once they go to bed with a man they feel committed, even though they know better. They find that contemporary customs, which so often make it difficult to establish relationships with men on a non-sexual basis, do not meet their real needs.

I see, therefore, strong male bias in all revisionist ethics which allow extensive sexual freedom. I appreciate the concern many authors have expressed for the values of love, care, concern for the rights and needs of partners. But if any of the authors advocating such positions have seriously considered the real psychology of women, their work eluded my extensive search of the relevant literature. They speak of persons, not of *men* and *women*. This blurs the very real differences between the two. Furthermore, in a society still strongly conditioned by the lingering effects of male supremacy, the point of view arrived at by such a strategy is bound to be primarily masculine. If there is one standard of what it is to be human—in this case *personhood*—the standard chosen can hardly be feminine, since women are only just beginning to figure out what their own standards are. I do not think it will be safe to talk about *personhood* until we know far more about *womanhood* than we now do, and until mature *womanhood* and *manhood* have been integrated into a concept which carries their common essence while respecting their differences.

I also believe that dualism itself, previously rejected on other grounds, is patriarchally conditioned. Men and women have very different attitudes to their bodies. Men, on the whole, tend to treat the body as a fancy power tool with which they can go out and subdue the environment, and they expect it to perform consistently on command. Women's connection to their bodies is integral, and the split between body and psyche is not natural for them. It is male gynecologists and psychiatrists who have decided that pre-menstrual syndrome is a disease, and that the emotional changes during and after pregnancy are to be viewed as instability.

Some of the sexual rules common in the past, especially the greater penalties imposed on women than on men for infractions, clearly derive from the view of women as property. These need no discussion since it is obvious that they have no place in a contemporary theology of sex.

Symbolic Issues

Reinhold Niehbuhr once said that our sacred myths need not be taken literally, but they must be taken seriously. The Genesis account vividly conveys the situation at the dawn of human consciousness, when our species first experienced the problems of moral choice. "And God said, Let us make Man in our own image. . .male and female created he them." The image of God contains elements which, though unified on the divine plane, are divided into two sexes on the human plane. Eve was to be Adam's *partner*. The inequalities between the sexes are a consequence of the Fall, directly attributable to Adam's refusal to take responsibility for eating the forbidden fruit. Instead, he pointed at Eve and said *"she* did it." Eve in turn said "no—the *snake* did it." They failed to stand *together* before God and say *"We* did it." This behavior broke the original perfect, trusting intimacy which God had given them, and set the pattern of wary mistrust of one sex toward the other. And this in turn led to the dissociation of the sexual instinct from its natural context of faithful, heterosexual intimacy.

The man/woman relationship is part of God's plan, the divinely given social basis for human community. To prevent our missing this point, the sexual metaphor is used throughout Scripture to describe God's relations with his people, Israel being the spouse of God, and the Church the Bride of Christ. When we are separate from God, we are not truly whole, and that fact is emphasized by such metaphors. The goal of Christian sexuality is not satisfaction, but completeness.[7]Either man alone or woman alone is only half of the image of God. We can find completeness only in the encounter with that which is radically *other*.

The divinely inspired author of the *Song of Songs* heads the list of those who, throughout the centuries, have understood that sexuality itself is a symbol of wholeness, of the reconciliation of opposites, of the loving at-one-ment between God and Creation. In the words of the great contemporary composer, Olivier Messaien (a devout Roman Catholic), "...the union of true lovers is for them a transformation on the cosmic scale."[8]

Confirmation of the symbolic importance of sex can be found in modern depth psychology, which draws on mythological sources as well as extensive investigation of individual men and women. Here is one of the most important differences between Freud and Jung. Storr describes it as follows: "Freud undoubtedly attributed supreme value to the orgastic release of sex, whereas Jung found supreme value in the unifying experience of religion. Hence Freud tended to interpret all numinous and emotionally significant experience as derived from, or a substitute for, sex." Insofar as modern sexology pays attention to psychology at all, it draws on this view. Storr continues: "...Jung tended to interpret even sexuality itself as symbolic, possessing 'numinous' significance in that it represented an irrational union of opposites and was thus a symbol of wholeness."[9] It is no accident that Freud is now perceived as suffering from patriarchal bias, while Jung from the start held that the masculine and feminine were co-valent principles, equally important.

This does not mean that persons who are celibate, either by choice or circumstance, cannot find wholeness. Friendships, relations with brothers, sisters and parents—these and many other encounters with the *other* can be psychologically and spiritually fruitful. Intercourse is the most intimate expression of interaction between the sexes, but it is, after all, only one. The problem with sex is that no other phenomenon of human existence can symbolize the vision of the sacramental universe in which all things are harmoniously connected, and at the same time manifest the tragic discontinuities which were inflicted on us and our world through the Fall. No other human activity so lends itself to subtle, as well as obvious, exploitation of self and of others. When sex is dissociated from its natural symbolic context, such exploitation is at least likely, perhaps inevitable.

Homosexuality

There is a considerable range of theological opinion about homosexuality. The various positions depend largely on the issues discussed above. Those who find personalist ethics convincing will
have no trouble fully accommodating at least some forms of homosexuality. The same is true of those who do not agree with my discussion of the symbolic significance of sexuality. They will not
sympathize with my concern that homosexuality supports patriarchy,
thereby postponing the achievement of real harmony and balance
between masculine and feminine. In *principle* homosexuality is a
radical discontinuity between the sexes, one which is only superfi-
cially different from the discontinuity inherent in the notion of male
supremacy, and which in many specific cases is actually derived
from that notion.

Some claim that homosexuality is a on a par with heterosexuality, that the human infant is sexually neutral at birth, and that therefore either sexual orientation is learned behavior. I believe this
goes too far. The evidence does not support so extreme a split between body and psyche. Heterosexuality is instinctive in all mam-
mals, and I see no reason to exclude human beings from that
general truth.

Raymond Lawrence believes that the principle of self-actualiza-
tion must be pre-eminent in constructing a new sexual ethics. He
believes that homosexuality is not intrinsically wrong. Nevertheless,
he says that ". . .the evidence seems weighted still in favor of the
bonded pair as the best hope for significant intimacy and the deep-
est emotional fulfillment. That marriage deserves the power of para-
digm is supported by the fact that man and woman are created a
mutually contingent pair. They must answer to each other for their
existence."[10] I agree.

Regardless of what role is assigned to homosexuality in the divine plan for human behavior, one thing is utterly clear. Any discrimination against, much less persecution of, anyone on the
grounds of sexual orientation alone is both spiritually and psychologically pathological. Immature and destructive expressions of sexuality exist in both homosexuals and heterosexuals, and society has
a right to intervene in such cases, as does the church. The homosexual orientation itself, however, even from the standpoint of the
most traditional theological position, can never be singled out for
special condemnation, nor does psychological research lend any
support to such emphasis. No matter what one's ethical standard

may be—conservative or liberal—everyone has violated it one way or another. We do not get to take the mote out of our brother's or sister's eye, ignoring the beam in our own.

Principles and Rules

There can be no quarrel with the basic principle governing sexual behavior, which is that *it is wrong to exploit others or to permit oneself to be exploited.* The rules expressing that principle have, as we saw in Chapter I, varied considerably, as has their enforcement. The function of such rules is to help maintain order in society. As the philosopher J.M. Cameron expresses it, "...in the past, modes of sexual behavior have been one thread in the web of culture, and the pattern and integrity of the web depend upon the disposition of every thread."[11] Nobody is challenging the principle, it is only the rules which are at issue.

The big problem is pluralism. We no longer believe that it is right for any one person or group to impose their ideas about how life should be lived on everybody else, especially not by force, but it is difficult to find a middle way between such oppression and the opposite pole of having few if any rules at all.

Rules are necessary because life without stable points of reference is impossible for most people, especially the young. Erikson, Piaget, Kohlberg and James Fowler have all shown that children and adolescents go through stages of living by rules, at first by adhering to them and later by rebelling against them. Unless this process takes place, the formation of secure personal identity is difficult—often impossible. This in turn prevents the development of autonomous adulthood, where conduct can be measured against an internalized and independently modified set of values. If you don't know where you are, you can't decide where to go from here, much less how to get there.

Unfortunately, as Paul Ramsey points out, "Ours is the only era in the entire history of human life on the planet in which the 'elders' of the tribe ask its newer members what the tribal rules and standards of expected behavior should be."[12] I believe this is an important factor in the rising popularity of fundamentalism, which has very strict rules. Many young adults, having suffered the chaos of parental indecisiveness during childhood, turn to fundamentalism with relief, sensing in it a compensation for the missing link in their development.

It is not always appreciated that the function of principles, and their expression in suitable rules, is to promote maximum flourishing of individuals so that they may contribute constructively to a wholesome community, one which supports everybody. If this were more widely understood, conservative clergy would not be so frightened of change, since they would no longer confuse rules with principles. Liberal clergy would not be so frightened of rules, but would recognize that they are always temporary, perhaps more so than usual in transitional times. Too many see rules as restrictive of freedom, and fail to understand the deeper truth contained in the Christian belief that perfect freedom is found *only* in the service of God.

The difficult problem of how to proclaim sexual rules in transitional times, knowing that responsible others will disagree, can only be solved if two things are kept in mind. First, one must be convinced that rules are necessary, at least for the young—and sometimes that means the spiritually young, not just the chronologically young.[13] Secondly, attention should be focused on principles, and this will leave room for changing one's mind about rules as the larger theological discussion progresses.

A good analogy is the problem of raising children in a neighborhood where other families do not have the same house rules. What do you say to your children then? You say: "These are the rules I believe in, and am therefore obligated to teach you; yes, I know the Joneses have different rules; the important thing is not the *content* of rules but their *existence*, since without rules you don't know where you are." You do not say that the Joneses are bad or stupid people because their rules are different. You do not say that all good parents have the same rules you do. You do not pretend that your rules are exactly the same as those of your ancestors. You are careful to give the reasons behind your rules. You give older children more latitude than younger ones in making their own decisions. Your goal is that they should become adults who are accustomed to considering both the theoretical significance and the practical consequences of their actions, rather than people who are canny enough to find rationalizations for "doing their own thing." You know that your success in reaching that goal does not depend on their deciding that all of your rules were right.

Rules We Should Keep

The summary of the Law says that we should love God with all our heart, soul, mind and strength, and our neighbors as ourselves. Now law is composed of rules of behavior, and yet, the summary of the Law does not mention rules. It does not even mention justice, which we might suppose to be the principle underlying laws. Instead, it declares that the absolute principle of behavior is love. St. Augustine knew that if we truly loved God with our whole being, it would be safe to do as we pleased since we would not please to do anything which might disturb the harmony of God's divine plan for our species. Nobody is able to love God perfectly. Many are unable to love others even moderately well, often because they cannot love themselves. This means that without realizing or intending it, we often exploit others or ourselves.

The evolution of consciousness, of culture, and of religious awareness shows increasing sensitivity to instances of exploitation. Among other things, this includes the growing realization that *everyone* is our neighbor. We can therefore no longer have any sexual customs which depend on the existence of a class of people whom we may treat with less care than we treat those in our familiar circle. Thus *the rule against prostitution is not only kept, but strengthened.*

Prostitution is usually defined in terms of whether or not money changes hands. This is not its essence. The essence is that another person is used to gratify sexual desires with no pretense of friendship and certainly no commitment. The encounter is not between two people, but between body parts. This obviously exploits the person of inferior status, usually (but not always) a woman. But it also exploits the patron, since he allows himself to be less than fully human, and treats not only his sexual partner but himself as a mere sexual object. These criticisms apply regardless of the gender or sexual orientation of the participants.

Any casual sexual encounter, heterosexual or otherwise, is subject to the same criticism. A common euphemism in the courts for sexual acts is to refer to them as "intimate." This is a gross misuse of the word, but the fact that it is so common shows that people intuitively know that sex *should* express true intimacy. Customs now current in many parts of society put pressure on people to engage in sexual acts as a condition of relationship. Such customs are mere variants of prostitution. Women are the usual victims, and many find that if they are not willing to have sex right away, they have no more dates. But it also occurs in some homosexual circles where the quick, impersonal sexual encounter is frequently sought by both parties.

In all of these instances the participants are exploiting one another and, perhaps less obviously, permitting themselves to be exploited. Men are less likely than women to perceive the self-exploitation since they have been socialized for the last twenty-five years to believe that frequent "hassle-free" sex is what they want. But they are incapacitating themselves for real intimacy, and the day will come when they will bitterly regret that. Thus *the rule against promiscuity of any kind is not only kept, but strengthened.*

The rule against adultery has two sources. One is the value of fidelity. The other is the plight of the third party. Couples who truly love one another, and are in a growth-promoting relationship of trusting intimacy, do not commit adultery.

Some years ago the O'Neills, in their book *Open Marriage*, proposed that "creative adultery" could strengthen a marriage. Later they wrote another book saying they had been wrong, and they got a divorce. It is perhaps true that if one member of a couple approaches a devoted spouse with a request for permission to have sex outside the marriage, the desire to please the loved one may produce an affirmative answer. But this is bound to break the intimacy, to be a blow to the self-esteem of the one who is—in the extremely apt popular phrase—"cheated on." Over time this initially minor crack in the marriage makes serious trouble. One way is by making the partners focus excessively on youthful appearance and physical desirability, at the expense of their full humanity. This is especially distressing to women who, in this culture, are already subject to that demeaning pressure. (A recent Clairol advertisement shows a man and a woman with gray hair, and the caption says "On him it's distinguished, on you it's just old.") Thus the adulterer always exploits his or her spouse whether that is immediately obvious or not.

The theological model is God's faithfulness to us. His interest in us is not capricious. The Bible often uses adultery as a metaphor to express the ways in which we are not faithful. But he always is. He does not commit "creative adultery," and when we try to imagine him doing so, the picture is ludicrous at least, perhaps even blasphemous. This should tell us clearly that any line of argument we may think up to justify human adultery is only a self-serving rationalization. In short, sin.

The third party in an adulterous relationship is also exploited. Adultery is often a bid for attention from the spouse when other means of communication have failed. In such cases the outsider is being used to express a need which is actually located between the spouses. In cases where one or both spouses feel no particular commitment to the marriage bond, but feel free to gratify their sexual needs according to personal whim, the behavior falls under the heading of promiscuity. Sometimes adultery is committed for the purpose of punishing the spouse, or of getting dominance over him or her. None of these motives has anything to do with the third person, who is, therefore, being exploited, especially since the adulterer usually returns to the spouse when the actual problem has been dealt with.

The right and wrong way to get divorced was discussed in Chapter III. Even in cases where marriage to the other person is intended following divorce, adultery is exploitation. The new person is being used as a springboard for escape from the marriage, and exposed to the risk of scandal and humiliation. Therefore, whether we are considering the value of fidelity or the status of the third party, *the rule against adultery is not only kept, but strengthened.*

In fact, I do not think it accidental that of all possible sexual irregularities, adultery is the one mentioned in the Ten Commandments. This speaks to its symbolic as well as its literal importance. Love, with its practical consequence of no exploitation, is the all-encompassing principle against which any proposed change must be tested. The Ten Commandments can usefully be thought of as ten second order principles which teach us how real love operates in various paradigmatic situations. While they all refer to concrete acts, they also have broad symbolic application to many aspects of life. Therefore, if I were asked to predict which rule I thought would always remain, no matter what society might be like several hundred years from now, I would unhesitatingly pick the rule against adultery.

It is worth remembering, however, that that commandment was given—and clearly understood—in a society which was polygamous. I therefore see the rule as prohibiting the breaking of the marriage bond *as that bond is constructed in a particular society.* This needs emphasis, since in many parts of the world—especially Africa—the Western objections to polygamy are not only irrelevant but sometimes even destructive. In the white population, the number of males and females is roughly equivalent. But in some black populations females outnumber males approximately three to one, even at birth. Many African Christians perceive white missionary insistence on monogamy more like cultural imperialism than true religion. We need to consider the possibility that genetic variables between populations may have influenced our customs more than we realize, making it possible for most people to find mates within an ordered social structure. Where women heavily outnumber men, we may expect polygamy. This is certainly morally preferable to female infanticide, which has been practiced in some places. Were there a population in which men heavily outnumbered women, we might expect polyandry. Where the numbers are roughly equal, monogamy is the result. In any case, the issue of adultery depends on the violation of the marriage bond, however that bond is defined and institutionalized.

Perversion

Some revisionists have argued that under certain circumstances such things as sado-masochism, incest, and sexual acts with children might be acceptable. Sado-masochistic practices between consenting adults are viewed as private contracts beyond condemnation by others. But the participants are using not only the bodies of others, but also their own bodies in the service of an unconscious compulsion. Such use is destructive of full humanity, and constitutes a wicked mockery of the proper use of sexuality, which should lead us toward, not away from, wholeness. Though the exploitation is mutual, it is exploitation nonetheless.[14]

It is impossible for children to give informed consent, particularly to their parents. Those who commit incest are exploiting their children in a peculiarly malignant way, since those children are unlikely to grow up without serious psychological damage even when the incest was not accompanied by violence or threats. Children lured into sexual activity by adults other than family members have a better chance of avoiding serious damage, since at least their capacity for basic trust—which depends on a proper relationship with the parents—is not also destroyed.[15]

Pornography is a form of perversion. The important concern about censorship is misapplied. Catherine MacKinnon, a law professor at Stanford University, provides an excellent argument when she says that

> "pornography is more act-like than thought-like. The fact that pornography. . .furthers the idea of the sexual inferiority of women, which is a political idea, doesn't make the pornography itself a political idea. . .Segregation expresses the idea of the inferiority of one group to another on the basis of race. That does not make segregation an idea. A sign that says 'Whites Only' is only words. Is it therefore protected by the First Amendment?"[16]

Evidence of connection between pornography and the rise in sex crimes is now undeniable, and that does not include the less obvious damage done to men whose attitudes to sex and therefore to women are negatively influenced. Since sex is social, not just private, anything which poisons the social atmosphere is contrary to religious principles.

All attempted defenses of any perverse behavior include the caution that "there must be no damage." Such judgement about damage suffers from a constricted time frame. People subjected to physical or psychological trauma in childhood often construct excellent defenses which permit them to live an apparently normal life for a time. But as life goes on, these defenses weaken and finally collapse. It is not unusual for anxiety and depression, sexual disorders, or other symptoms to manifest after a lapse of twenty or more years. I find all attempts to justify any of these practices psychologically naive. They are also cruel, since when such things are declared acceptable, those who suffer from them are deprived of the opportunity to do anything about relieving themselves of these dreadful burdens. J.M.Cameron puts the deeper, ultimately theological issues well:

> "...there is no feeling for the immensely old human tradition of venerating the powers of sexuality and hedging them about with taboos, myths, piety, an attitude for which the sexual is not an extra, a relaxation, a consolation, a relief of tension, though it may also be all these things, but a part of the sacred order of the cosmos...In the end the indictment of liberated sexuality...is that it makes sex trivial and empties life of its difficult mystery."[17]

Rules We May Re-examine

Creative rule-breaking is among the chief tools of moral progress. The story of Peter's dream, when he was told to eat flesh previously declared unclean, is a good example. The burden of proof is always on the rule-breaker. The discernment called for is that *rules should only be broken in the search for a more workable, subtler, or higher level expression of the principle which lies behind the rules.*

Are there any circumstances in which sexual activity outside of marriage is acceptable? It is certainly taking place—and not only in the exploitative situations enumerated above. In fact, it is so prevalent that many clergy simply shrug their shoulders, or turn a blind eye, thinking that there is nothing to be done about it anyway. Such things as engaged couples living together or older people, both single and widowed, having discreet affairs with other single people are ignored. But this way of handling these situations is not a good idea. It is really important to have thought these things through, otherwise clergy will be caught with nothing helpful to say when their advice, practical or moral, is sought. And, as we shall see, it is important to distinguish between pre-marital sex in the young and sex among older single people and the formerly married.

Fornication refers to single people and is thus distinct from adultery. A look at tradition does not support the widely-believed idea that our religion has always banned all cases of it. There are many passages in Scripture which, in English, forbid fornication. But that is a mistranslation of the word *pornea* which actually means prostitution.

A good case can be made for the idea that the prohibition is actually against any of the obviously exploitative sexual acts described earlier. Lawrence points out that the Torah does not prohibit fornication, and adds that in Jewish tradition coitus is a necessity and an obligation, ordered by God. "Nor is it restricted within monogamy. In thirteenth-century Spain, Nahmanides declared explicitly what is implicit elsewhere in Jewish tradition, that relations with an unattached woman are permissible. Sex is a sin only in the context of a broken promise, a betrayal of covenant, or an act of aggression or self-aggrandizement."[18]

The rule against any sex outside of marriage has been common. Conceding that Christianity suffered contamination from Greco-Roman dualistic beliefs as described in Chapter II, rules do not become prevalent unless they serve a purpose. The rule against pre-marital sex protected young women from exploitation by men whose immature sexuality was still dissociated. It also gave young men some incentive to grow up. The old custom of forcing men to marry despoiled virgins, especially if pregnant, prevented further exploitation and protected children. If these rules are to be relaxed, we must observe the principle of reducing exploitation.

Complete abolition of the rule would not serve that purpose. Psychiatric research warns against sexual experience at too early an age. The primary task of adolescence is to establish identity separate from parents, a personal set of values, and self-confident independence. Early sexual experience leads to prolonged adolescence by straining the ego's integrative capacity. The psychological damage appears to be worse for girls than for boys. This is only to be expected in view of the difference between male and female sexuality. We see that the old idea that girls need protection from uncontrolled male sexuality is correct, even though modern culture may call for different techniques of ensuring that protection. Boys also need protection, a fact not formerly recognized, and not recognized now by those who see nothing wrong with fixation of sex at the physical level. The necessary maturational task of learning to inte-

grate the physical sex drive with other personal and social aspects
of personality is made more difficult if boys are allowed from the
start to act out their sexual urges. We see that early sexual experience exploits both male and female adolescents, though in different
ways. So to prevent that, *at the very least we need a rule prohibiting
sex before the age of eighteen.*

After the age of eighteen, the situation changes. Courtship with a
view to marriage begins to occur. Personal, if not financial, independence from parents is well established by girls as well as boys. But
are they actually mature enough to make good, non-exploitative decisions about sex? The factors in our culture which prevent the desired level of maturity have already been discussed. In my experience most young people of that age do not have the necessary sub-
tlety or detachment to examine their own motives and feelings,
much less to assess correctly those of a proposed partner. Few
young men are able to spot the kind of young woman who has
been socialized to say "yes, dear" for fear of breaking the relationship, and who herself may not even know what she feels. And seldom have young men been trained to have the strength of character
to turn down an inviting sexual opportunity. Young women are
equally inept and frequently allow themselves to be exploited without realizing the true nature of the transaction until later. Others,
seeing how easy it is to manipulate a man through his sex drive,
take outrageous advantage of their partners. Most young people, especially males, do not realize that in selecting a partner for life,
deep friendship is the indispensable foundation.

It is not responsible to proclaim guidelines for personal deci-
sion-making, much less rules, unless these are fully explained.
Therefore, *in this culture, the church needs to provide education
about sexuality for adults as well as youth.* This is true regardless
of which standards clergy decide to espouse. Methods may vary, but
any system which stimulates or manipulates guilt or fear is bound
to fail. Emphasis should be on the positive values of the proclaimed
standard.

I recall an outstandingly successful program which began with a
weekend workshop for parents, dealing with marriage and family issues. This was followed the next weekend by a program for teenagers. The medical aspects of sex were discussed by a pediatrician
in the congregation. My part was to present the psychological and
spiritual aspects, importantly including the difference between male
and female sexuality, emphasizing that that difference was most pronounced at their age. Their chances of eventually selecting the right
mate would be enhanced if they could concentrate first on the
other tasks appropriate to their age group. I explained that those

tasks included learning how to develop friendships and assess emotional and mental compatibility—almost impossible to learn when relationships are prematurely short-circuited at the sexual level. Following this, there was a final session for parents and children together. Sexuality was presented as one of God's best gifts to us, which it was important to learn how to use wisely so that we could enhance both personal and community life and avoid doing harm. The minister and his staff had done a great deal of preparatory work before the program, with the result that over 80% of the congregation participated. Another parish tried to put on the same program, but the preparatory work was skipped and participation was poor.

What about people in their twenties or older who choose to live together? Many have been too involved in education or work to consider marriage. The strength of the sex drive is variable, and for some people total abstinence is cruel and unusual. Promiscuity and prostitution (paid or free) have been ruled out. Women now lead independent lives, no longer marrying from family or social pressure. They are also no longer raised to repress their own sexual drive. The contemporary solution is living together. Unfortunately, such relationships are often exploitative, at least subtly, usually of the woman. To avoid this, *at the very least we need a rule that one should not live with somebody one is in principle unwilling to marry.* Without such a rule, the chances are great that one or both partners are being used primarily as a sexual convenience. The rule becomes vital should a pregnancy occur. Many women have made the agonizing decision to have an abortion because the man responsible was someone unimaginable either as a husband or as a father. In other cases, the man felt that way about the woman or was simply refusing responsibility.

We need also to respect the decisions of young people who have been so unnerved by the prevalence of divorce in their parents' generation that they are unwilling to marry without testing the commitment by a time of living together. Such decisions are often based on a very high view of marriage. But Bejin, in an article on current extra-marital unions, points out that young people in such arrangements are unconsciously trying to "reconcile modes of behaviour that our ancient western society and most other cultures have traditionally found incompatible."[19] One must consider such experiments, conscientiously undertaken, as brave efforts to find new social structures, suited to the coming post-patriarchal era. It remains to be seen whether or not such efforts will in the long run prove viable. But young people involved in them should not be the object of Christian censure.

The case of extra-marital sex for older people, whether single or formerly married, is different only in detail. The principle of no exploitation remains. On the assumption that they are actually mature, not just older, allowances must be made for their greater experience in making decisions, including their ability to evaluate all the subtle factors about self and others which must be considered. However, clergy who form such sexual alliances themselves should remember that their lives are under scrutiny by the congregation, and they therefore run the risk that those unable to discriminate correctly in their own case may use the clerical example as a justification for inappropriate behavior.

The question of abortion is difficult. Most arguments make the error of supposing that in cases of problem pregnancy a right decision is possible. The irreversible mistake was made at conception. I have little patience either with the extreme "pro-life" position or with those who advocate abortion on demand. One of the marks of maturity is the recognition of times when the best that can be done is to choose the lesser evil. No two situations are exactly alike. The decision must be made far more quickly than is desirable about anything so important. The younger the woman, the more important it is to clarify her feelings, since it is not unknown for parents to pressure a daughter to have an abortion she desperately does not want, and which may haunt her in later life, in order to avoid scandal in the eyes of their own circle. I see no alternative but to deal with problem pregnancies case by case. Sin must sometimes be committed to avoid still greater sin. There are times, not limited to incest, rape or medical complications, when abortion is the least harmful solution. But *any decision for abortion is a special exception to the general rule that abortion is wrong.*

Finally, it is always important to consider the relation of sexual behavior to the total configuration of a person's life circumstances and state of emotional and spiritual maturity. The same act may mean very different things to different people, and may be progress in one case but regress in another. Consider the situation of someone deciding to live with a friend but with no intention of marriage. If the previous life was one of compulsive promiscuity, that is a step in the right direction. If, however, a married person has deserted spouse and children, and the new arrangement is just more fun, the moral judgement would be entirely different.

Conclusion

I have tried to present a way of thinking seriously about sexuality. The conclusions I have come to about particular forms of sexual expression may differ from those of many readers. My aim was primarily to describe how, rather than what to think, and I hope I have helped readers with that important task.

NOTES—CHAPTER IV

1. Philip Turner, *Sex, Money & Power*, (Cambridge, MA: Cowley Publications, 1985, p. 34).
2. ibid., p. 36.
3. ibid., p. 43.
4. ibid., p. 40.
5. Larry Dossey, M.D., *Space, Time and Medicine*, (Boulder, CO: Shambhala, 1982) and *Beyond Illness: Discovering the Experience of Health*, (Boston: Shambhala, New Science Library, 1984).
6. Ruth Tiffany Barnhouse, *Identity*, (Philadelphia, PA: The Westminster Press, 1984). See especially Chapter 5.
7. John Dixon, "The Sacramentality of Sex" in *Male and Female: Christian Approaches to Sexuality*, eds.: Ruth Tiffany Barnhouse and Urban T. Holmes, III, (New York: The Seabury Press, 1976).
8. Olivier Messaien, "Turangalila Symphony," Notes by the composer on record jacket, (New York: RCA LSC-7051, 1968).
9. Anthony C. Storr, *C. G. Jung*, (New York: Viking Press, 1973, p.13.
10. Raymond J. Lawrence, "Bench Marks for a New Sexual Ethics," *St. Luke's Journal of Theology*, March, 1985, Vol. XXVIII, No. 2, p.98.
11. J. M. Cameron, "Sex in the Head," *New York Review of Books*, May 13, 1976, pp. 19-28. This article is more than worth a special trip to the library.
12. Paul Ramsey, quoted by Lewis Penhill Bird, "What the Church Should Teach About Sex," *Christianity Today*, November 11, 1983, Vol. 27, No. 17.
13. James W. Fowler, *Stages of Faith*, San Francisco: Harper & Row, 1981.
14. Robert J. Stoller, *Perversion: The Erotic Form of Hatred*, (Washington, DC: American Psychiatric Press, 1986, paperback).
15. Karin Meiselman, *Incest: A Psychological Study of Causes and Effects*, (San Francisco: Jossey-Bass Publishers, 1978).
16. Catherine MacKinnon, in "Talk Back", *Common Cause Magazine*, September/October 1986, Vol. 12, No. 5., p.43. The entire section on pornography in this issue is worth a close look.
17. J. M. Cameron, *op. cit.*
18. Raymond J. Lawrence, "The Church and the Sexual Revolution," (Quarterly Review, Vol. 5, No. 1, Spring 1985, p.43).
19. Andre Bejin, "The Extra-marital Union Today" in *Western Sexuality*, eds. Philippe Aries and Andre Bejin, Tr. by Anthony Forster. (Oxford: Basil Blackwell, 1985).